# Governance and Public Management

Series Editor
Paul Joyce, INLOGOV, University of Birmingham, Birmingham, UK

*IIAS Series: Governance and Public Management*
International Institute of Administrative Sciences (IIAS)—*Setting the Governance Agenda Worldwide*
Website: http://www.iias-iisa.org
Edited by Paul Joyce

To cover the diversity of its members, the IIAS has set up four sub-entities:

- The EGPA (European Group for Public Administration)
- The IASIA (International Association of Schools and Institutes of Administration)
- The LAGPA (Latin American Group for Public Administration)
- The AGPA (Asian Group for Public Administration)

*Governance and Public Management Series*
This IIAS series of books on Governance and Public Management has a focus and breadth that reflects the concerns of the International Institute of Administrative Sciences. The Institute, which was set up in 1930, involves academics and governments from all around the world. The Institute's work involves supporting both practitioners and academics, which it does by encouraging the production of relevant knowledge on public governance and public management and by facilitating its dissemination and utilization.

It is the intention of the series to include books that are forward-looking, have an emphasis on theory and practice, are based on sound understanding of empirical reality, and offer ideas and prescriptions for better public governance and public management. This means the books will include not only facts about causes and effects, but also include ideas for actions and strategies that have positive consequences for the future of public governance and management. The books will offer a point of view about responses to the big challenges facing public governance and management over the next decade, such as sustainable development, the climate crisis, technological change and artificial intelligence (A.I.), poverty, social exclusion, international cooperation, and open government.

All books in the series are subject to Palgrave's rigorous peer review process: https://www.palgrave.com/gb/demystifying-peer-review/792492.

Caroline Howard Grøn · Anne Mette Møller

# Public Bureaucracy and Digital Transformation

Structures, Practices and Values

Caroline Howard Grøn
Department of Political Science
Aarhus University
Aarhus, Denmark

Anne Mette Møller
Department of Organization
Copenhagen Business School
Copenhagen, Denmark

ISSN 2524-728X      ISSN 2524-7298   (electronic)
Governance and Public Management
ISBN 978-3-031-67863-9      ISBN 978-3-031-67864-6   (eBook)
https://doi.org/10.1007/978-3-031-67864-6

© The Editor(s) (if applicable) and The Author(s), under exclusive license to Springer Nature Switzerland AG 2024

This work is subject to copyright. All rights are solely and exclusively licensed by the Publisher, whether the whole or part of the material is concerned, specifically the rights of translation, reprinting, reuse of illustrations, recitation, broadcasting, reproduction on microfilms or in any other physical way, and transmission or information storage and retrieval, electronic adaptation, computer software, or by similar or dissimilar methodology now known or hereafter developed.
The use of general descriptive names, registered names, trademarks, service marks, etc. in this publication does not imply, even in the absence of a specific statement, that such names are exempt from the relevant protective laws and regulations and therefore free for general use.
The publisher, the authors and the editors are safe to assume that the advice and information in this book are believed to be true and accurate at the date of publication. Neither the publisher nor the authors or the editors give a warranty, expressed or implied, with respect to the material contained herein or for any errors or omissions that may have been made. The publisher remains neutral with regard to jurisdictional claims in published maps and institutional affiliations.

Cover illustration: © John Rawsterne/patternhead.com

This Palgrave Macmillan imprint is published by the registered company Springer Nature Switzerland AG
The registered company address is: Gewerbestrasse 11, 6330 Cham, Switzerland

If disposing of this product, please recycle the paper.

# Acknowledgments

This book grew out of a five-year research project entitled "Replacing interaction? How ICT influences knowledge sharing and leadership in physically dispersed public organizations" (REPLACE), funded by the Independent Research Foundation Denmark (Grant No. 8091-00016B).

We are deeply grateful to everyone who helped make this book possible.

In particular, we wish to thank the third member of our research team, Mathilde Andreassen Winsløw, who conducted a significant amount of the fieldwork that provides the empirical foundation for this book. Thank you, Mathilde, for all your effort and contributions to the project and our team!

We also wish to thank our colleagues at Aarhus University and Copenhagen Business School for their encouraging comments and constructive feedback. We are particularly grateful to Peter Bjerre Mortensen and Mads Leth Jakobsen, who both took valuable time to provide detailed comments on a very early draft and helped guide our efforts. We also thank Sylvester Grünberger Tønnesen for his help in preparing the manuscript for publication.

Finally, we would like to thank everyone we came across in the two agencies where we conducted our fieldwork, not least of all the front-line workers and managers who allowed us to observe them and ask all kinds of questions about their everyday work. Thank you for opening your doors to us. We could never have done this without you!

# Contents

1 **Introduction: Studying Public Bureaucracies under Digital Transformation** — 1
 1.1 Why Study Public Bureaucracies Under Digital Transformation? — 3
  1.1.1 Overview of Findings — 5
 1.2 Public Bureaucracies as Object of Inquiry — 8
  1.2.1 Public Bureaucracies and Bureaucratic Values — 10
 1.3 Unpacking the Concept of Digital Transformation — 12
 1.4 Research Approach — 15
  1.4.1 Research Design — 16
  1.4.2 Methods and Data — 17
 1.5 The Structure of the Book — 21
 References — 21

2 **Division of Labor and Hierarchy in the Digitalized Bureaucracy** — 27
 2.1 Division of Labor in the Digitalized Bureaucracy — 29
  2.1.1 Division of Labor Between Humans and Systems: Working the In-Between — 31
  2.1.2 Division of Labor Between the Operative Core and the IT Organization: Bridging the Gaps — 38
 2.2 Hierarchy in the Digitalized Bureaucracy — 46

|  |  | 2.2.1 | What Managers Do in the Digitalized Bureaucracy | 46 |
| --- | --- | --- | --- | --- |
|  | References |  |  | 56 |
| 3 | Rules, Programmability, and Discretion in the Digitalized Bureaucracy |  |  | 57 |
|  | 3.1 | Rules and Programmability in the Digitalized Bureaucracy |  | 60 |
|  |  | 3.1.1 | Programming Human Behavior | 60 |
|  |  | 3.1.2 | Beyond Programmability: Dealing with Residuals | 62 |
|  |  | 3.1.3 | When Instructions Fall Short: The Need for a Human Touch | 64 |
|  | 3.2 | Discretion in the Digitalized Bureaucracy |  | 66 |
|  |  | 3.2.1 | The Changing Nature of Discretionary Decision-Making | 66 |
|  |  | 3.2.2 | Frontline Discretion in the System-Level Bureaucracy | 70 |
|  |  | 3.2.3 | Upholding the Bureaucratic Ethos | 74 |
|  | References |  |  | 80 |
| 4 | The Public Bureaucracy Under Digital Transformation |  |  | 83 |
|  | 4.1 | Division of Labor |  | 84 |
|  | 4.2 | Hierarchy |  | 86 |
|  | 4.3 | Rules and Programmability |  | 87 |
|  | 4.4 | Discretion |  | 88 |
|  |  | 4.4.1 | Bureaucratic Values Under Digital Transformation? | 91 |
|  | 4.5 | Concluding Remarks |  | 94 |
|  |  | 4.5.1 | Understanding Competences and Context in the Digitalized Bureaucracy | 95 |
|  |  | 4.5.2 | The Production and Reproduction of the Digitalized Bureaucracy | 97 |
|  | References |  |  | 99 |

References 101

Index 109

# About the Authors

**Caroline Howard Grøn** is Associate Professor at the King Frederik Center for Public Leadership in the Department of Political Science, Aarhus University. Her research centers on public leadership, public management, organization theory, and the digital transformation of public organizations.

**Anne Mette Møller** is Associate Professor in the Department of Organization, Copenhagen Business School. Her research focuses on public management and leadership, policy implementation, frontline work, professional knowledge and practice, digitalization, and organizational ethnography.

# List of Vignettes

| | |
|---|---|
| Everything I'm doing here is on paper | 29 |
| Setting the alarm | 31 |
| That is some workaround! | 32 |
| Clean-up duty | 34 |
| What constitutes a problem? | 35 |
| Construction site meeting | 38 |
| Technical or human error? | 40 |
| Some of us have no prerequisites | 41 |
| Lost in organization | 42 |
| Technically, there is nothing wrong | 44 |
| What is acceptable? | 45 |
| A black hole | 47 |
| Only managers | 48 |
| Not authorized | 49 |
| 100% control | 50 |
| Playing support right | 51 |
| It just has to work! | 51 |
| Missing antennae | 53 |
| Information overload | 54 |
| Most of it runs really well | 60 |
| It would be great to clear it out | 62 |
| We make decisions | 67 |
| Calibrating discretion | 68 |
| Don't get too comfortable | 69 |
| It would be stupid to submit the evidence | 70 |

Do you want my children to go hungry? 71
Answering the phone 72
Many still just write an email 75
We are the tax agency—we should be able to explain it! 76
You still have to print everything 77

# List of Figures

| | | |
|---|---|---|
| Fig. 1.1 | Analytical framework | 16 |
| Fig. 2.1 | How digital technologies enable and constrain division of labor | 46 |
| Fig. 2.2 | How digital technologies enable and constrain hierarchy | 55 |
| Fig. 3.1 | How digital technologies enable and constrain rules and programmability | 66 |
| Fig. 3.2 | How digital technologies enable and constrain discretion | 80 |
| Fig. 4.1 | How digital technologies enable and constrain public bureaucratic values | 94 |

# LIST OF BOXS

Box 1.1    Characteristics of the Weberian bureaucracys    10
Box 1.2    Public bureaucratic values    12

# List of Tables

Table 1.1  Overview of cases  18
Table 1.2  Overview of fieldwork  19
Table 1.3  Overview of methods and data  20

CHAPTER 1

# Introduction: Studying Public Bureaucracies under Digital Transformation

**Abstract** Digitalization has changed the face of bureaucracy. This book aims to give an in-depth analysis of how digital transformation enables and challenges public bureaucracies and the values associated with this particular form of organization. This introductory chapter presents an overview of the book's main findings and presents the theoretical and methodological foundation for the analytical chapters. The theoretical framework is developed through discussions of the characteristics and features associated with the book's central concepts: public bureaucracy and digital transformation. The research approach is based on an interpretive and practice-based methodology. Data was generated through organizational ethnography in two highly digitalized government agencies in Denmark (the Tax Agency and the Agricultural Agency). Across our analyses, we find that digital technologies both reduce and increase the complexity of the public bureaucracy: Digital technologies enable a smoothly running bureaucratic machine while simultaneously creating snags in this machine. Digital technologies hence play paradoxical role in their interplay with the bureaucracy.

**Keywords** Public bureaucracy · Digital transformation · Bureaucratic values · Practice-based methodology · Organizational ethnography

Most casework in the tax agency is digitalized. However, only one unit has all their archives digitized—the others are still working on it. The goal is for all case files to be accessible through digital systems in the near future. Until recently, the agency stored everything on paper. Some case files, such as land registry documents, are centuries old. Documents worthy of preservation are sent to a giant building in another town with file cabinets from floor to ceiling. Sometimes it feels like a loss, frontline worker Karen says. Her co-worker agrees: It is a piece of history, after all, when you hold those yellowed documents in your hands. Viewing them on the screen is not the same thing.

(Field notes, The Danish Tax Agency)

Agricultural inspector Jane tells me about the agency's current efforts to introduce "administrative control" on grasslands. Instead of conducting physical inspections, they now use satellite images to determine whether there has been sufficient activity on the field, e.g., mowing or grazing. This is a condition for farmers to receive a subsidy. If the satellite-based calculation indicates no activity, the farmer receives a letter. They then have 14 days to withdraw the field from their subsidy application or submit documentation of activity (photos) via an app. But it is difficult to evaluate this documentation, Jane explains. In her experience, it is almost impossible to assess where the photos were taken. It depends a lot on the quality of farmers' devices. Often, they use mobile phones with poor GPS to take photos, and there is absolutely no order to it when they submit them. "You would think that you can make the assessment," says Jane, but in her view, "you just can't when you haven't been out there physically." Still, this is the direction the agency wants to go: fewer physical controls.

(Field notes, The Danish Agricultural Agency)

Traditional images of bureaucratic organizations feature small offices with filing cabinets along the walls and large desks adorned with piles of paper. Digitalization, however, has changed the face of bureaucracy. Today, bureaucrats can work from anywhere and carry their department's entire filing system everywhere they go, as long as they have a laptop and their phone. They move around virtual paper piles but seldom need to touch actual paper. They rely on digital case management systems and can share and send files between hierarchical levels and across organizational boundaries with one click.

Street-level bureaucrats are becoming screen-level bureaucrats. Soon, agricultural inspectors may no longer need to get in their cars and drive out on physical inspections, but can stay in the office and look at photos on a screen that farmers have submitted through an app. Instead of meeting farmers face-to-face, they communicate via email and digital case management systems. Citizens no longer have to submit four signed copies of their request or wait in line in hallways outside a bureaucrat's door. Instead, they are required to use digital self-service systems and are just as likely to communicate with the IT helpdesk or a chatbot as with the bureaucrat deciding on their case.

In short, bureaucrats today face a brave new world, where the technical and material aspects of bureaucratic life are changing along with the ways in which cases are processed and decisions made. Digitalization eases access to data and facilitates communication, but it also affects the substance of what public bureaucracies—and the people who work in them—actually do, including internal workflows and functions, routines and procedures, and interactions with citizens and stakeholders. Digitalization also adds different layers of complexity, as public bureaucracies increasingly rely on the expertise of IT professionals. Indeed, digitalization appears to influence all aspects of the public bureaucratic organization and thereby one of the foundation stones on which our societies stand. Building on these observations, **this book aims to give an in-depth analysis of how digital transformation enables and challenges public bureaucracies and the values associated with this particular form of organization.**

## 1.1 Why Study Public Bureaucracies Under Digital Transformation?

The idea that societies are going through a "digital transformation" (Scupola and Mergel 2022; Cortellazzo et al. 2019) has formed the basis for extensive research in public as well as private organizations in recent decades. Yet the influence of digitalization and digital transformation on bureaucratic organizations as such has not received much attention in this literature (Eom 2022). In her 2023 book, Pahlka goes so far as to argue that:

Digital work, which in our larger society commands so much attention (whether it's lionized or vilified), in government is reduced to an afterthought. It's not what important people do, and important people don't do it. They hand it off to people many rungs down the ladder, or to companies hired to do it for them. At times it almost seems that status in government is dependent on how distanced one can be from the implementation of policy (Pahlka 2023, 15).

While Pahlka's statement may not reflect the situation in all governments and agencies, there is no question that the influence of digitalization on government and on the bureaucratic form of organization calls for more focused attention, including from scholars. To date, the ways in which digitalization is transforming public bureaucracies remain underexplored. This book contributes to this important task. It is important to underscore that we do not consider digital transformation to be a positive or negative development per se, nor a deterministic or an uncontrollable one, as the concept of "transformation" may lead one to assume. Rather, we use the word to indicate the already ubiquitous role of digital technologies in public bureaucracies, which is likely to increase in the future. Whether such a development is good or bad for public bureaucracies is still an open question. Yet we also believe that if we are to exploit the benefits of digital transformation and avoid detrimental pitfalls, we need to gain a better understanding of what digital transformation means for public bureaucracies.

To address our research question, we dive deeply into the inner workings of two highly digitalized government agencies in Denmark, which is considered one of the most digitalized countries in the world (OECD 2024). Drawing on ethnographic fieldwork among frontline workers and managers, we offer an unprecedented view into everyday life in the digitalized bureaucracy and use this to develop a nuanced understanding of what digitalization means for bureaucratic organizations. While we ground our discussion of the digital transformation of public bureaucracies in close observations of everyday practice, we simultaneously seek to trace the dynamics through which the institutional context influences and is influenced by the constraints and affordances of digital technologies.

Unlike much current research on digital transformation (e.g., Schuilenburg and Peeters 2021; Meijer et al. 2021), we do not engage with more recent developments in relation to algorithmic predictions and artificial intelligence. Rather than focusing on experimental development projects and rare instances of radical transformation, we focus our attention on those digital technologies that are already an integral part of organizational life in the two agencies we study, i.e., "everyday technologies" and their implications for bureaucratic practices and public bureaucracies as such. Our rich empirical data enables us to analyze how participants—i.e., managers and employees in the two agencies—experience and adjust to the affordances and constraints of particular digital technologies as well as the broader ecology of technologies on which their work depends, and to examine how this affects their tasks as well as the enactment of public bureaucratic values in practice. We hereby gain a deeper understanding of how the ongoing digital transformation enables and constrains the bureaucratic organization in ways that may bring about institutional change.

### 1.1.1 Overview of Findings

Before diving deeper into the theoretical background for our study, we provide a brief overview of our most central findings. Overall, our analysis shows how digital transformation may both enhance and challenge central features of public bureaucratic organizations: Digital technologies enable a smoothly running bureaucratic machine while simultaneously creating snags in this machine. In this way, digital technologies play a paradoxical role in their interplay with the public bureaucracy. As we expand on below, we focus our analysis on central characteristics of bureaucratic organizations, namely division of labor, hierarchy, rules and programmability, and bureaucratic discretion, as well as key bureaucratic values such as legality, transparency, responsiveness, and accountability.

- In relation to *division of labor*, we find that digitalization enables handling of large caseloads and allows frontline workers to focus on critical or atypical cases. Frontline workers adjust their work around systems, connect systems that do not communicate, rectify mistakes in automated case processing, and compensate when systems are dysfunctional. The division of labor between digital systems and humans is continuously negotiated in complex interactions among frontline workers, managers, process owners, IT developers, and legal experts, thereby challenging traditional divisions of labor between different parts of the organization. Bridging

the gap between the operative core and IT functions is an ongoing task.
- In relation to *hierarchy*, we find that digitalization constrains managerial roles, as frontline managers rarely possess knowledge and expertise regarding actual case processes or the operation of digital systems. Instead, the managerial role shifts toward digital gatekeeping and digital caretaking, where managers control employees' access to digital systems and facilitate the availability and functionality of software and hardware. In interactions between frontline workers, process owners, and IT developers, managers tend to occupy more passive roles, while the IT organization appears to cut across the traditional hierarchy.
- In relation to *rules and programmability*, we find that digital technologies enable standardization and automatization of tasks and encourage detailed scripting of non-automated tasks as well. Still, there are limits to standardization and programmability. Parallel and informal systems are created to deal with the overflow of cases that do not fit in the digital systems. Some cases are too complex for automated decision-making, but even programmable casework is sometimes challenged by technical failure, suboptimal digital systems, or missing hardware. In these situations, humans are needed to keep operations running.
- In relation to *bureaucratic discretion*, we find that frontline workers in the digitalized bureaucracy still exercise bureaucratic discretion, communicate with citizens, and engage in emotional labor, including in digitally mediated encounters. In cases where processing has been automated, frontline workers' opportunities for exercising discretion are clearly constrained. Instead, these opportunities reside in the complex and indeterminate interactions between frontline workers, managers, process owners, IT developers, and legal experts, who deal with cases in "batches" rather than individually. Rather than being expert decision-makers, frontline workers enact discretion as digital mediators and sometimes take on time-demanding digital detective work to answer citizens' questions and help them navigate the digitalized bureaucracy.
- In relation to *public bureaucratic values*, we find that digital technologies enable bureaucracies to process large numbers of cases in standardized ways that—in principle—ensure *transparency, accountability, efficiency,* and *legality*. Digital systems discipline managers,

employees, and citizens into a framework that (ideally) reflects the legal basis for their interactions as well as principles of sound administration. This allows humans to direct their attention to critical or atypical cases, whereby digital technologies also enable bureaucratic *responsiveness*. At the same time, digital technologies constrain the enactment of bureaucratic values. Increasing organizational complexity, fragmentation, and cross-cutting hierarchies tend to constrain transparency and efficiency and blur accountability, while highly complex legal frameworks and frequent changes in rules and regulations challenge the legality of digitalized operations. In this setting, frontline workers seek to safeguard bureaucratic values as they engage in problem-solving with managers and IT functions. In their encounters with citizens, they (sometimes) enact responsiveness by serving as *digital guides* and engaging in *digital detective work*, yet their ability to do so is hampered by the unintelligibility and intransparency of automated processes.

We explore these findings and discuss their implications in more detail in the following chapters. At this point, we wish to highlight two general observations: First, our findings suggest that both individual digital technologies and the digitalized public bureaucracy as such are in a state of *permanent reconstruction*. We therefore end our book with a call for a more processual understanding of digital government. Rather than a journey or a destination, digital transformation is perhaps best understood as a *mode of organizing* that both perpetuates well-known organizational challenges and introduces new ones. Importantly, many of the challenges we observe are not likely to be overcome, but must be handled on an ongoing basis.

Second, our findings show that frontline workers and managers play key roles in taking on these challenges. Digitalization is sometimes associated with de-skilling and a reduced need for human labor. By contrast, our findings show that a variety of human skills are needed to manage and navigate the plethora of digital systems and tools that make up the digitalized bureaucracy. This suggests that, rather than de-skilling, digital transformation entails a need for *re-skilling*. Our findings highlight the importance of cultivating both *practical expertise* and a strong *bureaucratic ethos* among frontline workers and managers to enable them to continuously enact and protect public bureaucratic values in everyday practice.

Our empirical analysis calls attention to the need to safeguard public bureaucratic values in the digital age. We are not alone in raising this concern (e.g., Widlak et al. 2021; Røhl 2022 [2023]). It is our hope that this book will contribute to current debates about what it takes to ensure good governance in the digital age. Based on our analyses, we invite the reader to consider how the opportunities presented by the continuous development of digital systems and tools may be utilized in ways that support key values of democratic public bureaucracies.

In the following sections, we outline the conceptual landscape of the book. We first discuss the concepts of public bureaucracies, the bureaucratic organization, and bureaucratic values. We then discuss the concepts of digital transformation and digital technologies and seek to outline different strands of the vast literature around these concepts, focusing in particular on public organizations. Toward the end of the chapter, we introduce our research approach and empirical material in more detail and present an outline of the rest of the book.

## 1.2 Public Bureaucracies as Object of Inquiry

Central to our argument is the observation that many (most) public organizations are bureaucracies (Perrow 1986; du Gay 2000). Perrow argued that "…where all organizations strive towards efficiency as defined by their owners, the rational-legal form of bureaucracy is the most efficient form of administration known in industrial societies" (Perrow 1986, 4). As we move beyond the industrial age, bureaucracy is still the most common form of organization in both the public and the private sector (Monteiro and Adler 2022).

We find bureaucracies in many places in the public sector whose characteristics resemble the ideal type of organization put forward by Weber (1978): Clear hierarchical structures are commonplace, just as the work is often highly regulated by abstract rules such as legislation or internal codes of conduct (Taskin and Edwards 2007). We further find extensive division of labor and specialization of organizational units (for example, a unit in the tax agency deals exclusively with taxes related to motor vehicles, while a unit in the agricultural agency is specialized in inspections of organic cattle). Such functions are based on professional expertise, and recruitment and advancement are based on merit. Written communication and documentation are essential. Further, employees must exercise neutrality and keep their professional and personal lives separate.

These ideal characteristics of bureaucracy are well known and likely recognizable to many readers. However, the concept of bureaucracy is multifaceted and warrants further discussion. In their recent review, Monteiro and Adler (2022) identify three different analytical perspectives on bureaucracy in the scholarly literature: bureaucracy as an organizing principle (e.g., du Gay 2000), bureaucracy as a paradigm (e.g., March and Simon 1993; Blau 1956), and bureaucracy as a type of organizational form (e.g., Mintzberg 1980). The first perspective understands bureaucracy as the organizational manifestation of a more fundamental principle. Depending on the reading (or translation) of Weber's original texts on bureaucracy, the most important principle is taken to be either instrumental rationality, value rationality, or domination. The second perspective understands bureaucracy as the "paradigm of modern organization," which is then characterized as either dysfunctional or flexible. The third perspective is rooted in contingency theory, where bureaucracy is one type of organization among others.

Our approach in this book aligns most closely with the first perspective, as we view public bureaucracies as organizational manifestations of fundamental principles related to both legal-instrumental and value-based rationality. We use the term "public bureaucracy" to denote organizations that embody key characteristics of the Weberian ideal type of bureaucracy (Weber 1978) and are situated in a public context where democratic government and the rule of law prevail. In other words, we do not consider bureaucracy merely as an *instrument* of policy implementation but also as an *institution* (Olsen 2006).

Box 1.1 outlines the characteristics of the Weberian bureaucracy that are central to our analysis. Notably, we do not see these features as immutable. One example concerns the link between authority and professional expertise. In the Weberian bureaucracy, a higher standing in the hierarchy of authority is an expression of superior professional knowledge and expertise (Monteiro and Adler 2022; Møller et al. 2022). While this link is not always evident in later conceptualizations of bureaucracy, our analysis here suggests that this link is also no longer evident in practice. This is perhaps one of the most significant implications of the digital transformation for public bureaucracies (we return to this discussion in Chapter 4). In the following, we elaborate on our understanding of the value component of public bureaucracies

> **Box 1.1 Characteristics of the Weberian bureaucracy**
>
> - Formalized division of labor
> - Hierarchy
> - Based on abstract rules
> - Reliance on written communication
> - Recruitment based on merit; often requiring theoretical knowledge (e.g., law)
> - Full time employment and clear division between personal and professional life
>
> (Weber 1978; Jespersen 1996).

### 1.2.1 Public Bureaucracies and Bureaucratic Values

While the bureaucratic form of organization exists in private organizations as well, our interest here is in public organizations, which have been found to differ from their private counterparts on several accounts (Boyne 2002; Boye et al. 2022). One important difference between public and private bureaucracies relates to the particular values that public bureaucracies are expected to uphold, which in turn has implications for the digital transformation of public bureaucratic organizations. Values can be understood as "a conception, explicit or implicit, distinctive of an individual or characteristic of a group, of the desirable which influences the selection from available modes, means and ends of action" (Kluckhohn 1951, 395). While values according to this definition are conceptions held by individuals or a group, much scholarship on bureaucracy views this way of organizing as instilled with certain values, which the people who work in them are socialized into sharing (du Gay 2000; Olsen 2006). This is especially true in a public, democratic context.

Weber studied the bureaucratic form of organization primarily in the context of government agencies, and so, in addition to the principles mentioned above, the *instrumental rationality* of bureaucracy is strongly associated with the *rule of law*, as these laws codify the goals and procedures of public organizations (Monteiro and Adler 2022). As argued by

Olsen (2006), bureaucracy can be seen as an institution by which administration is based on "the rule of law, due process, codes of appropriate behavior, and a system of rationally debatable reasons" and as "part of society's long-term commitment to a *Rechtsstaat* and procedural rationality for coping with conflicts and power differentials" (Olsen 2006, 3).

The principle of *value rationality* entails that, although the legal-instrumental rationality is dominant, and bureaucrats are required to follow orders based on the hierarchy of authority, they are also committed to value and substantive rationality by way of their bureaucratic ethos (du Gay 2000). This implies that a decision is rational if it is in accordance with a higher-order goal. Accordingly, bureaucrats should not blindly implement decisions, but rather react if these decisions "seem incorrect or at variance with the mission of their office or the wider organization" (Monteiro and Adler 2022, 435). Indeed, Olsen argues, bureaucracy has "legitimate elements of nonadaptation" to leaders' orders and environmental demands, as bureaucrats are first and foremost bound "to obey, and be the guardians of, constitutional principles, the law, and professional standards." If these are at risk of being violated, bureaucrats can be expected to "speak truth to power" (Olsen 2006, 3). In line with this view, bureaucratic values can also be seen as linked to a bureaucratic ethos that is shaped by the particular public office in question and (ideally) guides bureaucrats in their actions (du Gay 2000; Møller et al. 2022).

However, while we may agree on the central role of values in principle, the issue quickly becomes more difficult in practice. Determining precisely which values are central to public bureaucracies is not straightforward, as illustrated in the public administration literature, which has continuously taken an interest in public values (Bozeman 2007; Jørgensen 2007; Bryson et al. 2015). In 2007, Jørgensen and Bozeman provided a public value inventory that identified 72 public values, which makes it clear that public organizations are quite value-dense. For our purposes here, we focus on a limited number of values (see Box 1.2) that are broadly recognized as central to public bureaucracies, namely legality, efficiency, responsiveness, transparency, and accountability (see, e.g., Bovens and Zouridis 2002; Douglas and Meijer 2016; Jørgensen and Bozeman 2007; Olsen 2006; Røhl 2022 [2023]; Zacka 2017). These values played a significant role in the two government agencies we studied, and we observed them both directly (e.g., on screensavers) and indirectly as constituting important aspects of participants' bureaucratic ethos.

Further, to determine the concrete meaning of abstract values in relation to particular cases or circumstances in practice requires conscious consideration and deliberation. While this is often considered the prerogative of actors at the top of the hierarchy of authority (Monteiro and Adler 2022), scholars have argued that such value-based judgment in practice often falls on so-called street-level bureaucrats, i.e., bureaucrats who interact directly with citizens in the course of their work (Lipsky 2010). In other words, value conflicts in practice often need to be resolved by those at the bottom of the hierarchy (Zacka 2017). Following this observation, our empirical investigation is focused on street-level bureaucrats and frontline managers.

> **Box 1.2 Public bureaucratic values**
>
> - Legality
> - Efficiency
> - Responsiveness
> - Transparency
> - Accountability
>
> (Weber 1978; Olsen 2006; Jørgensen and Bozeman 2007; Zacka 2017).

## 1.3 Unpacking the Concept of Digital Transformation

Public organizations use numerous digital technologies in their daily work. Digital documents and spreadsheets, email and calendars, instant messaging services (chats) and online meetings, digital file sharing, case management systems, and intranet are all commonplace in Danish public bureaucracies and in organizations around the world. Generic software exists alongside digital systems developed for, or adapted to, local purposes, including digital self-service systems aimed at citizens and stakeholders. In the two government agencies from which this book draws its empirical material, the latter includes software that allows taxpayers to register and control their own tax information, and software that allows producers of flowers and plants to register their exports within the EU. Examples of software for internal use include Geo Information Systems (GIS), which allows employees to access maps that show, e.g., land ownership. The list could go on and on. In sum, digitalization is and has been changing public bureaucracies in several ways in recent decades, to the extent that it seems relevant to speak of a *digital transformation*.

Whereas *digitization* denotes conversion from analog to digital form, e.g., digitizing physical archives, *digitalization* includes a change in processes and demands new competences from employees. In contrast, the concept of *digital transformation* has a more encompassing nature. Mergel and colleagues propose that digital transformation is best viewed as a holistic effort to revise core government processes that *"evolves along a continuum of transition from analog to digital to a full stack review of policies, current processes, and user needs and results in a complete revision of the existing and the creation of new digital services"* (Mergel et al. 2019, 12). Others have suggested that digital transformation denotes a situation where digital systems and tools have taken on an *"infrastructural"* character (Cortellazzo et al. 2019, 2).

An example of the relevance of this perspective is the 2022 breakdown of the Danish public identification system NemID, which for a period of 4 days kept 1.5 million citizens from accessing services such as their public health records and personal tax information and even from borrowing books at their public library. At the same time, attorneys nationwide were kept from accessing their cases, as the system used by the Danish Courts was also linked to NemID and was made inaccessible during the breakdown.[1] Just as a power outage can put a stop to most work in a government agency, so can lack of access to digital systems or breakdowns in their functionality. As some tasks, e.g., case processing, may essentially consist of accessing information in one system and combining it with information from another, lack of access may prove completely detrimental to workflow, even when this goes unnoticed by the broader public.

In the public administration literature, digital transformation has generally been studied either in terms of macro-level change, i.e., as a

---

[1] https://www.dr.dk/nyheder/indland/stribevis-af-fejl-op-til-nemid-nedbrud-der-lam mede-advokater-og-borgerservice-vi.

continuous transformation of society and government , or in terms of micro-level change, i.e., the increased integration of digital tools into individual and organizational practices and routines. Researchers have long taken an interest in the system-changing nature of digitalization and conceptualized the ongoing transformation under headings such as *e-government*, *digital era governance*, *digital transformation*, and the *digital twin bureaucracy* (Dunleavy et al. 2006; Yildiz 2007; Scupola and Mergel 2022; Eom 2022). Some contributions focus on the promises of increased digitalization (Dunleavy et al. 2006; Wirtz and Birkmeyer 2015), while others present critical reflections on why digitalization initiatives fail (Anthopoulos et al. 2016) and discuss a variety of unintended consequences (Buffat 2015; Bovens and Zouridis 2002; Prokop and Tepe 2022).

At the same time, the public administration literature has seen an increase in case studies that focus on individual technologies, such as the implementation of management accounting and electronic patient record systems in hospital settings (Padovani et al. 2014; Hansen and Nørup 2017), or studies of particular IT platforms or information-sharing systems (e.g., Boersma et al. 2012; Shah et al. 2019). Others have examined how IT systems support governance structures, for example in relation to the 2013 flooding of the German city of Passau (Wittmann et al. 2015), and still others have studied the determinants of the use of intranet and e-services (Wang and Feeney 2016). These contributions help us understand the digital transformation of public bureaucracies and their services on the micro-level, but they also appear as more or less isolated pieces in a larger puzzle. Individual digital technologies are typically used as part of a broader ecology of artifacts (Bødker and Klokmose 2012), which means that their uses and importance are contingent on the presence and use of other technologies within and across organizational boundaries.

In sum, the extant literature provides important knowledge about the processes and actors involved in digital transformation on both macro- and micro-levels, but few attempt to bridge the two. Further, many studies of digital transformation processes are based mainly on interviews (e.g., Mergel et al. 2019; Edelmann et al. 2023; Scupola and Mergel 2022), or survey data (Barrutia and Echebarria 2021; Tangi et al. 2020), and tend to address either descriptive questions such as which actors are involved in the digital transformation (Scupola and Mergel 2022; Gabryelczyk 2020), or prescriptive questions such as what competences are needed to manage digital transformation (Edelmann et al. 2023). With this book, we add a different perspective to this bourgeoning literature, as we seek to develop a deeper and more nuanced understanding of how digitalization is transforming the public bureaucracy *as such*, focusing on its central characteristics and values as outlined above.

## 1.4 Research Approach

So far, we have outlined our understanding of the characteristics and values associated with the public bureaucracy and discussed the multifaceted nature of digital transformation. In this section, we present our research approach in more detail.

Our research approach is open-ended in the sense that we do not set out to test hypotheses. Rather than attempting to theorize a priori about how digitalization transforms the public bureaucracy, we take an abductive approach (Schwartz-Shea and Yanow 2012), in which we anchor our empirical investigation and analysis in extant theory and concepts. In other words, we ground our argument in extant theory but develop it via a thorough empirical investigation of "bureaucracy in action" (Monteiro and Adler 2022, 428). This approach allows us to explore what the digitalized public bureaucracy looks like and feels like in everyday practice, and to use our observations as an opportunity to engage in practice-based theorizing (Feldman and Orlikowski 2011). To generate data for our project, we employ organizational ethnography (Ybema et al. 2009), as this allows us to consider the entire ecology of digital systems and tools that permeate the two agencies and to pay attention to the social and material as well as technical aspects of digital technologies as they are used in everyday practice (Orlikowski 1992; Mergel et al. 2019).

Analytically, we seek to bridge macro- and micro-level perspectives on digital transformation by focusing on the link between everyday practices and the public bureaucracy-as-institution (Olsen 2006). This approach is rooted in an understanding of practices as social actions that produce and reproduce the social structures that in turn constrain and enable actions—what Giddens (1984) referred to as *structuration* (see also Feldman and Orlikowski 2011; Nicolini 2013). This translates into an interest in social actors' "doings and sayings" and the extent to which these doings and sayings have some kind of recurrence and express generalized rules or perceptions of appropriateness (Schatzki 2005, 2006]). In this way, we

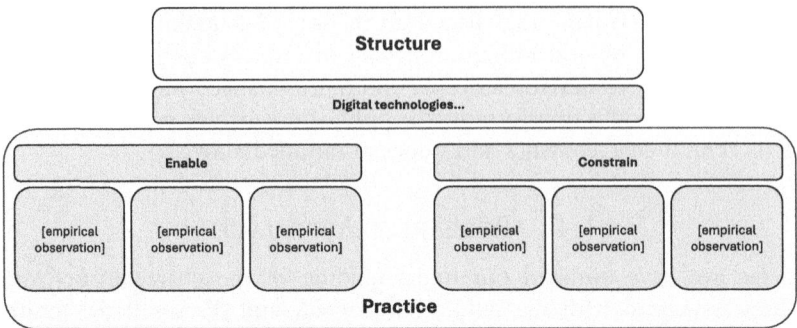

Fig. 1.1 Analytical framework

seek to shed light on the ways in which a particular institutional structure—the public bureaucracy in a Western democracy—shapes the uses and interpretations of technologies in everyday practice and is also continuously reinterpreted and transformed by these very practices (Barley and Orlikowski 2001).

Throughout the book, we illustrate our findings using different versions of Fig. 1.1 below, as we analyze how digital technologies enable or constrain practices, empirically observed, within the domain of various structural components of the bureaucratic organization. Specifically, we focus on the following elements: division of labor and hierarchy (Chapter 2), rules, programmability, and discretion (Chapter 3), and bureaucratic values (Chapter 4). We expand on our methods and data in the next section.

### 1.4.1  Research Design

Our analysis is based on ethnographic fieldwork in two Danish government agencies: the Danish Tax Agency and the Danish Agricultural Agency. Denmark is one of the most digitalized countries in the world and is generally considered a global frontrunner when it comes to digitalization of government operations (OECD 2024). The Tax Agency and the Agricultural Agency are both classic public bureaucracies in their organization, and both have important regulatory tasks vis-à-vis citizens. The two agencies are among the most digitalized organizations in Danish government; both employ large numbers of IT professionals, and case processing and public encounters depend completely on digital systems and tools. Moreover, employees in both agencies have the opportunity to work remotely, meaning that telework and online meetings are an integrated part of everyday practice. Our empirical material hence constitutes a "most likely" case, which allows us to explore the implications of an extensive and (relatively) mature digital transformation of public bureaucracies. An overview of the characteristics of the two agencies is presented in Table 1.1.

It is worth noting that we do not propose to analyze the process of digital transformation in terms of what has *changed*, i.e., the difference between "then" and "now." Rather, we present an in-depth investigation of what the digitalized public bureaucracy looks like at this moment in time. As such, our analysis may serve as an indication of what an increasingly digitalized future entails for public bureaucracies, thereby serving as a relevant reference point beyond the Danish context. At the same time, we are aware that what we observe in these agencies is also an artifact of particular historical decisions and developments. We draw our conclusions and discuss the implications of our analysis with this in mind.

### 1.4.2 Methods and Data

Our research approach reflects our ambition to study "bureaucracy in action" in the digital age. Accordingly, we are interested in the everyday practices and actual work carried out by frontline workers and managers in the two agencies rather than abstract descriptions of roles, tasks, responsibilities, and procedures (Brown and Duguid 1991), just as we aim to gain an in-depth understanding of digital technologies-in-use (Orlikowski 1992) rather than abstract descriptions of their intended uses and effects. To support this ambition, we applied an ethnographic approach, which revolved around shadowing (Czarniawska-Joerges 2007) of frontline workers and managers in various units in the two agencies as well as qualitative interviews.

In short, we shadowed four frontline managers as well as four employees who worked for the observed managers in each agency, amounting to a total of 16 key research participants. We followed each key participant for 3 days and observed them as they carried out their everyday tasks. This involved sitting or standing next to them at their desks, participating in meetings both physically and online, having lunch with co-workers, listening in on informal conversations in the office as

Table 1.1 Overview of cases

| | Agricultural agency | Tax agency |
|---|---|---|
| Core tasks | Policy implementation, regulation, and inspection of the agriculture sector, and administration of Danish and EU subsidies | Ensure correct taxation and correct and timely payments of taxes and debts |
| Citizen interaction | Yes—with farmers, gardeners, agriculture consultants, and others Interaction during physical inspections + communication via telephone and email | Yes—with all taxpayers (citizens, non-citizens, private companies, associations, etc.). Interaction via email, telephone, or integrated in digital case management systems |
| Content of frontline work | Physical and administrative inspections, provision of certificates, land negotiations, and guidance on rules and regulations | Case processing, communication of decisions, guidance on rules and regulations, and use of self-service systems |
| Frontline workers' professional backgrounds | Agricultural specialists, land surveyors, gardeners, and veterinarians | Tax specialists, bankers, bookkeepers, accountants, office trainees, and unskilled workers |
| Digitalization | Highly digitalized, external providers, as well as in-house development of new digital systems, employ a high number of IT staff | Highly digitalized, external providers, as well as in-house development of new digital solutions, employ the highest number of IT staff in Danish government |
| Locations | Locations in Copenhagen, Southern Denmark, and five regional offices; inspectors work from their home office, regional office, or the field | Locations in Copenhagen and many other places all over the country; employees may work from home 1 – 2 days per week |

well as telephone conversations with citizens (in the tax agency), and participating in physical inspection visits to farmers and others (in the agricultural agency). Participants were selected from different units in each of the two agencies: four different units in the tax agency and three different units in the agricultural agency. In the tax agency, all four units were located at the same address. In the agricultural agency, units were located in regional offices across the country (one of the selected units spanned two regional offices). We thus carried out fieldwork in five different locations. In total, our data consists of 47 days of observations amounting to 327 hours (see Table 1.2).

In addition to our observations, we carried out 39 interviews (28 individual interviews and 11 group interviews) with a total of 49 participants. We interviewed shadowed participants both before and after fieldwork. The interview data further includes group interviews with additional frontline workers in each of the selected units as well as interviews with directors in both agencies. Interviews lasted between 30 and 90 minutes. At the end of each day, we transcribed our field notes into full texts to make them comprehensible and meaningful to all researchers in the team. We also added our immediate reflections on the observations and

Table 1.2 Overview of fieldwork

| Participants | No. of days | No. of hours |
| --- | --- | --- |
| **Fall 2021: The Danish tax agency** | | |
| Section 1.1: Manager | 3 | 25 |
| Section 1.1: Employee | 3 | 22 |
| Section 1.2: Manager | 3 | 21 |
| Section 1.2: Employee | 3 | 22 |
| Section 1.3: Manager | 3 | 20 |
| Section 1.3: Employee | 3 | 21 |
| Section 1.4: Manager | 3 | 23 |
| Section 1.4: Employee | 3 | 21 |
| **Tax agency total** | **24 days** | **175 hours** |
| **Winter 2022: The Danish agricultural agency** | | |
| Section 1.1: Manager | 2 | 13 |
| Section 1.1: Employee | 3 | 18 |
| Section 1.1: Manager | 2 (1 online) | 17 |
| Section 1.1: Employee | 3 | 14 |
| Section 1.2: Manager | 2 | 21 |
| Section 1.2: Employee 1 | 3 | 20 |
| Section 1.2: Employee 2 | 1 | 3 |
| Section 1.3: Manager | 3 | 23 |
| Section 1.3: Employee | 3 | 17 |
| Seminar for section 1.1, 1.2, and 1.3 | 1 | 6 |
| **Agricultural agency total** | **23 days** | **152 hours** |
| **Fieldwork total** | **47 days** | **327 hours** |

provided a full overview of the day's events, added photos, etc. All interviews were recorded and transcribed. All data was imported into NVivo and coded through several iterative processes involving all members of the research team. The analyses and examples in this book are all derived from this extensive material. An overview of methods and data is provided in Table 1.3. For a detailed discussion of methodological foundations, considerations, and details regarding our research approach, see Møller (2023) and Winsløw (forthcoming).

**Table 1.3** Overview of methods and data

| Data source | Agricultural agency | Tax agency | Total |
| --- | --- | --- | --- |
| **Observations** | 23 days of shadowing: 5 frontline workers + 4 frontline managers in 3 units (4 geographical locations) | 24 days of shadowing: 4 frontline workers + 4 frontline managers in 4 units (1 geographical location) | 47 days/ 327 hours 7 units/ 5 locations |
| **Individual and group interviews** | 4 group interviews with shadowed participants (pre-fieldwork) 8 individual interviews with shadowed participants (post-fieldwork) 3 individual interviews with directors 3 group interviews with 13 additional frontline workers | 8 individual interviews with shadowed participants (pre-fieldwork) 8 individual interviews with shadowed participants (post-fieldwork) 1 individual interview with director 4 group interviews with 16 additional frontline workers | 28 individual interviews 11 group interviews 49 different participants |
| **Additional meetings** | 1 introductory meeting with higher-level managers, 2 online meetings with participating units (preliminary findings + member checking) | 1 intro meeting with director + all frontline managers, 2 online meetings with participating units (preliminary findings + member checking) | 6 meetings |

## 1.5 The Structure of the Book

In this chapter, we have presented a set of arguments as to why the ongoing digital transformation of public bureaucracies warrants further investigation. We provided a summary of our findings and presented the theoretical and methodological foundations for our study. In the coming chapters, we discuss our empirical analyses in detail, with the purpose of showing how the characteristics and values of public bureaucracies are constrained and enabled by digital technologies.

Chapter 2 focuses on the elements of division of labor and hierarchy, while Chapter 3 focuses on rules, programmability, and discretion. In both of these chapters, we begin by briefly introducing the structural elements in focus before turning to our empirical analysis. In Chapter 4, we summarize the main results of the preceding analyses and discuss the implications of our findings with regard to the enactment of bureaucratic values. We end with some concluding remarks and reflections on future avenues for research.

Throughout the analytical chapters, we use short vignettes from our observation data to support, elaborate upon, and illustrate our arguments. The vignettes are closely based on our field notes, and all present situations and conversations that we observed directly in the field, sometimes lightly reworked to include, e.g., relevant contextual details. Quotation marks ("") indicate that participants are quoted verbatim. In addition to grounding our analytical reflections in empirical observations, the vignettes serve to provide the reader with a nuanced impression of everyday life in the digitalized bureaucracy. All vignettes are provided with a title (e.g., "Setting the alarm"), and we refer to the different vignettes by their titles as we move along in our argument. The front matter of the book contains an overview of all vignettes so that readers can easily locate the vignettes referred to throughout the text.

## References

Anthopoulos, Leonidas, Christopher G. Reddick, Irene Giannakidou, and Nikolaos Mavridis. 2016. Why E-Government Projects Fail? An Analysis of the Healthcare. Gov Website. *Government Information Quarterly* 33 (1): 161–173. https://doi.org/10.1016/j.giq.2015.07.003.

Barrutia, Jose M., and Carmen Echebarria. 2021. Effect of the COVID-19 Pandemic on Public Managers' Attitudes toward Digital Transformation.

*Technology in Society* 67: 101776. https://doi.org/10.1016/j.techsoc.2021. 101776.
Blau, Peter M. 1956. *Bureaucracy in Modern Society*. New York, NY: Crown Publishing Group/Random House.
Bødker, Susanne, and Clemens Nylandsted Klokmose. 2012. "Dynamics in Artifact Ecologies." In *Proceedings of the 7th Nordic Conference on Human-Computer Interaction: Making Sense Through Design, NordiCHI '12*, 448–57. New York, NY: ACM.
Boersma, Kees, Pieter Wagenaar, and Jeroen Wolbers. 2012. "Negotiating the 'Trading Zone'. Creating a Shared Information Infrastructure in the Dutch Public Safety Sector." *Journal of Homeland Security and Emergency Management* 9 (2), 1–25. https://doi.org/10.1515/1547-7355.1965
Bovens, Mark, and Stavros Zouridis. 2002. From Street-Level to System-Level Bureaucracies: How Information and Communication Technology is Transforming Administrative Discretion and Constitutional Control. *Public Administration Review* 62 (2): 174–184. https://doi.org/10.1111/0033-3352.00168.
Boye, Stefan, Rebecca Risbjerg Nørgaard, Emily Rose Tangsgaard, Mathilde Andreassen Winsløw, and Mathias Rask Østergaard-Nielsen. 2022. Public and Private Management: Now, Is There a Difference? A Systematic Review. *International Public Management Journal* 27 (2): 109–142. https://doi.org/10.1080/10967494.2022.2109787.
Boyne, George A. 2002. Public and Private Management: What's the Difference? *Journal of Management Studies* 39 (1): 97–122. https://doi.org/10.1111/1467-6486.00284.
Bozeman, B. 2007. *Public Values and Public Interest: Counterbalancing Economic Individualism*. Washington, DC: Georgetown University Press.
Brown, John Seely, and Paul Duguid. 1991. "Organizational Learning and Communities-of-Practice: Toward a Unified View of Working, Learning, and Innovation." *Organization Science* 2 (1), 40–57.
Bryson, John M., Barbara C. Crosby, and Laura Bloomberg, eds. 2015. *Public Value and Public Administration*. Washington, DC: Georgetown University Press.
Buffat, Aurélien. 2015. Street-Level Bureaucracy and E-Government. *Public Management Review* 17 (1): 149–161. https://doi.org/10.1080/14719037. 2013.771699.
Cortellazzo, Laura, Elena Bruni, and Rita Zampieri. 2019. "The Role of Leadership in a Digitalized World: A Review." *Frontiers in Psychology* 10, 1–21.
Czarniawska-Joerges, Barbara. 2007. *Shadowing: And Other Techniques for Doing Fieldwork in Modern Societies*. Malmö, Sweden; Herndon, VA; Oslo: Liber; Copenhagen Business School Press; Universitetsforlaget.

Douglas, Scott, and Albert Meijer. 2016. Transparency and Public Value—Analyzing the Transparency Practices and Value Creation of Public Utilities. *International Journal of Public Administration* 39 (12): 940–951. https://doi.org/10.1080/01900692.2015.1064133.

Du Gay, Paul. 2000. *In Praise of Bureaucracy: Weber, Organization, Ethics*. London: SAGE Publications Ltd

Dunleavy, Patrick, Helen Margetts, Simon Bastow, and Jane Tinkler. 2006. New Public Management Is Dead—Long Live Digital-Era Governance. *Journal of Public Administration Research and Theory* 16 (3): 467–494. https://doi.org/10.1093/jopart/mui057.

Edelmann, Noella, Ines Mergel, and Thomas Lampoltshammer. 2023. Competences That Foster Digital Transformation of Public Administrations: An Austrian Case Study. *Administrative Sciences* 13 (2): 44. https://doi.org/10.3390/admsci13020044.

Eom, Seok-Jin. 2022. The Emerging Digital Twin Bureaucracy in the 21st Century. *Perspectives on Public Management and Governance* 5 (2): 174–186. https://doi.org/10.1093/ppmgov/gvac005.

Feldman, Martha S., and Wanda J. Orlikowski. 2011. Theorizing Practice and Practicing Theory. *Organization Science* 22 (5): 1240–1253. https://doi.org/10.1287/orsc.1100.0612.

Gabryelczyk, Renata. 2020. Has COVID-19 Accelerated Digital Transformation? Initial Lessons Learned for Public Administrations. *Information Systems Management* 37 (4): 303–309. https://doi.org/10.1080/10580530.2020.1820633.

Giddens, Anthony. 1984. *The Constitution of Society: Outline of the Theory of Structuration*. Berkeley: University of California Press.

Hansen, M.B., and I. Nørup. 2017. Leading the Implementation of ICT Innovations. *Public Administration Review* 77 (6): 851–860. https://doi.org/10.1111/puar.12807.

Jespersen, Peter Kragh. 1996. *Bureaukratiet: Magt og effektivitet*. København: Djøf Forlag.

Jørgensen, Torben Beck. 2007. Public Values, their Nature, Stability and Change. The Case of Denmark. *Public Administration Quarterly* 30 (4): 365–398. https://doi.org/10.1177/073491490703000401.

Jørgensen, Torben Beck, and Barry Bozeman. 2007. Public Values: An Inventory. *Administration & Society* 39 (3): 354–381. https://doi.org/10.1177/0095399707300703.

Kluckhohn, Clyde. 1951. "Values and Value-Orientations in the Theory of Action: An Exploration in Definition and Classification." In *Toward a General Theory of Action*, edited by T. Parsons and E. A. Shils, 388–433. Cambridge, MA: Harvard University Press.

Lipsky, Michael. 2010. *Street-Level Bureaucracy: Dilemmas of the Individual in Public Services. 30th Anniversary.* Expanded. New York: Russell Sage Foundation.

March, James Gardner, and Herbert Alexander Simon. 1993. *Organizations*, 2nd ed. New York: John Wiley & Sons.

Meijer, Albert, Lukas Lorenz, and Martijn Wessels. 2021. Algorithmization of Bureaucratic Organizations: Using a Practice Lens to Study How Context Shapes Predictive Policing Systems. *Public Administration Review* 81 (5): 837–846. https://doi.org/10.1111/puar.13391.

Mergel, Ines, Noella Edelmann, and Nathalie Haug. 2019. Defining Digital Transformation: Results from Expert Interviews. *Government Information Quarterly* 36 (4): 101385. https://doi.org/10.1016/j.giq.2019.06.002.

Mintzberg, Henry. 1980. Structure in 5's: A Synthesis of the Research on Organization Design. *Management Science* 26 (3): 322–341. https://doi.org/10.1287/mnsc.26.3.322.

Møller, Anne Mette. 2023. "Inside the Digital State: Frontline Workers and Digital Transformation of Government." Paper presented at the Public Management Research Conference (PMRC), Utrecht University, The Netherlands, June 27–30.

Møller, Anne Mette, Kirstine Zinck Pedersen, and Anja Svejgaard Pors. 2022. The Bureaucratic Ethos in Street-Level Work: Revitalizing Weber's Ethics of Office. *Perspectives on Public Management and Governance* 5 (2): 151–163. https://doi.org/10.1093/ppmgov/gvac001.

Monteiro, Pedro, and Paul S. Adler. 2022. Bureaucracy for the 21st Century: Clarifying and Expanding Our View of Bureaucratic Organization. *Academy of Management Annals* 16 (2): 427–475. https://doi.org/10.5465/annals.2019.0059.

Nicolini, Davide. 2013. *Practice Theory, Work, and Organization: An Introduction.* Oxford: Oxford University Press.

OECD. (2024). *2023 OECD Digital Government Index: Results and Key Findings.* OECD Public Governance Policy Papers, January 30. https://www.oecd.org/en/publications/2023-oecd-digital-government-index_1a89ed5e-en.html.

Olsen, Johan P. 2006. Maybe It Is Time to Rediscover Bureaucracy. *Journal of Public Administration Research and Theory* 16 (1): 1–24. https://doi.org/10.1093/jopart/mui027.

Orlikowski, Wanda J. 1992. The Duality of Technology: Rethinking the Concept of Technology in Organizations. *Organization Science* 3 (3): 398–427.

Orlikowski, Wanda J., and Stephen R. Barley. 2001. Technology and Institutions: What Can Research on Information Technology and Research on Organizations Learn from Each Other? *MIS Quarterly* 25 (2): 145. https://doi.org/10.2307/3250927.

Padovani, Emanuele, Rebecca L. Orelli, and David W. Young. 2014. Implementing Change in a Hospital Management Accounting System. *Public Management Review* 16 (8): 1184–1204. https://doi.org/10.1080/14719037.2013.792383.
Pahlka, Jennifer. 2023. *Recoding America: Why Government Is Failing in the Digital Age and How We Can Do Better*. New York, NY: Metropolitan Books.
Perrow, Charles. 1986. Economic Theories of Organization. *Theory and Society* 15 (1–2): 11–45. https://doi.org/10.1007/BF00156926.
Prokop, Christine, and Markus Tepe. 2022. Talk or Type? The Effect of Digital Interfaces on Citizens' Satisfaction with Standardized Public Services. *Public Administration* 100 (2): 427–443. https://doi.org/10.1111/padm.12739.
Røhl, Ulrik B. U. 2022. *Automated, Administrative Decision-Making and Good Administration. Friends, Foes, or Complete Strangers?* PhD diss.: Aalborg University Press, Aalborg.
Røhl, Ulrik B. U. 2023. Automated Decision-Making and Good Administration: Views from inside the Government Machinery. *Government Information Quarterly* 40 (4): 101864. https://doi.org/10.1016/j.giq.2023.101864.
Schatzki, T.R. 2005. Peripheral Vision: The Sites of Organizations. *Organization Studies* 26 (3): 465–484. https://doi.org/10.1177/0170840605050876.
Schatzki, T.R. 2006. On Organizations as They Happen. *Organization Studies* 27 (12): 1863–1873. https://doi.org/10.1177/0170840606071942.
Schuilenburg, Marc, and Rik Peeters, eds. 2021. *The Algorithmic Society: Technology, Power, and Knowledge*. London; New York: Routledge/Taylor & Francis Group.
Schwartz-Shea, Peregrine, and Dvora Yanow. 2012. *Interpretive Research Design: Concepts and Processes*. E-book version. New York, NY: Taylor & Francis Ltd.
Scupola, Ada, and Ines Mergel. 2022. Co-Production in Digital Transformation of Public Administration and Public Value Creation: The Case of Denmark. *Government Information Quarterly* 39 (1): 101650. https://doi.org/10.1016/j.giq.2021.101650.
Shah, Tejal, Louise Wilson, Nick Booth, Olly Butters, Joe McDonald, Kathryn Common, Mike Martin, Joel Minion, Paul Burton, and Madeleine Murtagh. 2019. Information-Sharing in Health and Social Care: Lessons from a Socio-Technical Initiative. *Public Money & Management* 39 (5): 359–363. https://doi.org/10.1080/09540962.2019.1583891.
Tangi, Luca, Marijn Janssen, Michele Benedetti, and Giuliano Noci. 2020. "Barriers and Drivers of Digital Transformation in Public Organizations: Results from a Survey in the Netherlands." In *Electronic Government. Lecture Notes in Computer Science*, edited by G. Viale Pereira, M. Janssen, H. Lee, I. Lindgren, M. P. Rodríguez Bolívar, H. J. Scholl, and A. Zuiderwijk, vol. 12219, 42–56. Cham: Springer International Publishing.

Taskin, Laurent, and Paul Edwards. 2007. The Possibilities and Limits of Telework in a Bureaucratic Environment: Lessons from the Public Sector. *New Technology, Work and Employment* 22 (3): 195–207. https://doi.org/10.1111/j.1468-005X.2007.00194.x.

Wang, S., and M.K. Feeney. 2016. Determinants of Information and Communication Technology Adoption in Municipalities. *American Review of Public Administration* 46 (3): 292–313. https://doi.org/10.1177/0275074014553462.

Weber, Max. 1978. *Economy and Society: An Outline of Interpretive Sociology.* Edited by G. Roth, and C. Wittich. Berkeley: University of California Press.

Widlak, Arjan, Van Eck Mariles, and Rik Peeters. 2021. "Towards Principles of Good Digital Administration: Fairness, Accountability and Proportionality in Automated Decision-Making." In *The algorithmic society: technology, power, and knowledge, Routledge studies in crime, security and justice,* edited by M. Schuilenburg and R. Peeters. London; New York: Routledge/Taylor & Francis Group.

Winsløw, Mathilde Andreassen. forthcoming. *Leadership in Digitalized Public Organizations* (working title). PhD diss., Aarhus University School of Business and Social Sciences Graduate School.

Wirtz, Bernd W., and Steven Birkmeyer. 2015. Open Government: Origin, Development, and Conceptual Perspectives. *International Journal of Public Administration* 38 (5): 381–396. https://doi.org/10.1080/01900692.2014.942735.

Wittmann, Sebastian, Marlen Jurisch, and Helmut Krcmar. 2015. Managing Network Based Governance Structures in Disasters: The Case of the Passau Flood in 2013. *Journal of Homeland Security and Emergency Management* 12 (3): 529–569. https://doi.org/10.1515/jhsem-2014-0078.

Ybema, Sierk. 2009. *Organizational Ethnography: Studying the Complexities of Everyday Life.* Los Angeles: SAGE.

Yildiz, Mete. 2007. E-Government Research: Reviewing the Literature, Limitations, and Ways Forward. *Government Information Quarterly* 24 (3): 646–665.

Zacka, Bernardo. 2017. *When the State Meets the Street: Public Service and Moral Agency.* Cambridge, MA: The Belknap Press of Harvard University Press.

CHAPTER 2

# Division of Labor and Hierarchy in the Digitalized Bureaucracy

**Abstract** This chapter focuses on two central tenets of the bureaucratic organization: division of labor and hierarchy. By analyzing how digitalization shapes the daily work of frontline workers and managers in the two agencies, the chapter shows how digital technologies support, enable, and challenge traditional hierarchies and division of labor with important implications for the enactment of public bureaucratic values such as transparency, legality, and accountability.

**Keywords** Public bureaucracy · Digital systems · Division of labor · Hierarchy · IT professionals · Authority · Expertise

In this chapter we provide an analysis of how digitalization shapes the daily work of frontline workers and managers with the aim of showing how digital technologies support, Enable, and challenge traditional hierarchies and division of labor in the two agencies

Division of labor is central to Weber's (1978) argument regarding rational authority: to make the best possible decisions, everyone cannot master everything. Rather, a rational order must depend on division of labor, allowing certain actors to focus on only smaller parts of the whole and build expertise. A similar logic can also be found in the writings

© The Author(s), under exclusive license to Springer Nature Switzerland AG 2024
C. H. Grøn and A. M. Møller, *Public Bureaucracy and Digital Transformation*, Governance and Public Management, https://doi.org/10.1007/978-3-031-67864-6_2

of Durkheim (2008; see also Freudenburg, 1993), when he argues for organic solidarity in a society with increased specialization. In later organization theory, March and Simon (1993) similarly point to the importance of division of labor. In a situation with limited cognitive resources, individuals depend on division of labor within organizations to attempt solutions to problems that are not only "satisficing" but moving toward optimal (Simon 1982). In other words, division of labor is considered a prerequisite for qualified decision-making in complex organizations.

Specialization can be organized according to a range of different principles; Gulick (1937), for example, famously presented four P's: purpose, place, persons, and process. Each of these categories may define how division of labor is organized. However, as division of labor increases, so does the risk that organizations will not coordinate their efforts. Division of labor hence also creates vulnerability in complex systems and increases the need for coordination (Freudenburg 1993). Coordination is ensured by hierarchy, a second central defining feature of bureaucracy.

Hierarchy is a form of organization where relations are defined in terms of superiority and subordination according to the formal structure of the organization. The hierarchy indicates how authority is distributed within the organization. According to Weber, the most developed form of bureaucracy is a monolithic hierarchy (Weber 1997). Hierarchy is necessary in situations where decisions cannot be programmed, i.e., when decisions cannot be made solely by following the legal basis on which an organization operates. In such situations, lower organizational echelons need the ability to leave decision-making to higher organizational echelons. Just as division of labor allows for functional specialization across units, hierarchy allows for a kind of functional division of labor between lower and higher organizational echelons.

While the issues that move up within an organization may differ from context to context, Foss and Klein (2014) point out that the involvement of higher organizational echelons is particularly important in situations where decisions have to be made quickly, where they demand organizational overview, or where there is a need for coordination between different parts of the organization. However, as Galbraith (1977) points out, highly hierarchical organizations are at risk of overloading their hierarchies if too many decisions need to be pushed up to higher organizational echelons.

In the following sections, we first provide some empirical insights into what division of labor looks like in a digitalized bureaucracy and how digital technologies enable and constrain division of labor. Second, we take a close look at how digital technologies affect the hierarchical order.

## 2.1 Division of Labor in the Digitalized Bureaucracy

On a first glance, division of labor in the two agencies is, quite traditionally, defined by the functional separation of different aspects of the tasks performed by the two agencies (related to, e.g., inspections of different types of animals, or organic farming, or the administration of different types of taxes, or private or corporate citizens). However, alongside this unsurprising division of labor, other divisions of labor appear when focusing on the digitalized nature of the two agencies: first, between digital systems and employees, and second, between the operative core and the IT development functions. Notably, these divisions of labor appear to be less clear and to be negotiated on an ongoing basis. In the following sections, we explore these different aspects of division of labor. However, before diving into these matters, we wish to highlight some features of the context for our study that should be kept in mind when reading the analyses in this and the following chapters.

First, as noted in Chapter 1, our ambition in this book is to show *how things are* rather than how they have changed. Still, the fact that they used to be different is an important backdrop for our analysis. Both the tax agency and the agricultural agency have been extensively digitalized in recent decades. Yet in "Everything I'm doing here is on paper," we get a glimpse of the cumbersome administrative procedures in the non-digitalized bureaucracy that still exists in some areas.

---

**Everything I'm doing here is on paper**

*We spend most of the afternoon at one of the big plant export companies. After having conducted a routine inspection in the hall, we walk to the back office, where stacks of documents—certificates for plant exports—await agricultural inspector Arnold's arrival. Arnold explains there are often more than 40 certificates with attachments, which must be approved before export. He sighs at the thought. He says that the company has developed its own IT system to create certificates; it is much more advanced than the agency's.*

*The documents lie in piles on an otherwise empty desk, ready for checking, signing, and stamping. Arnold hangs his jacket on a chair, sits down comfortably at the desk, and opens a small bag containing stamps. One has his signature for use on copies, to avoid manual signing on each document. The second stamp is the agency's logo—a green circle with text around the edge and a crown in the center—to signal official approval. The last stamp is for approving copies of originals and is labelled "copy-confirm." Arnold selects a smaller stack of documents and expertly flips through them with confident hand and finger movements. He briefly checks tables, looks for additional statements, and ensures their presence in the annexes. He signs, stamps, adds dates in some places. While Arnold stamps away, young women keep running to his desk to fetch small stacks of already processed documents. After an hour, Arnold holds up a document to show me: "This one has over 30 annexes, so I split it up a bit; otherwise, you can easily forget a stamp." After an hour and a half, he is done. "It's a lot of signatures on a day like this," he says, and adds that he really appreciates his stamps. At least he does not have to write his signature by hand.*

*Later in the car, Arnold remarks that I haven't seen much digitalization today: "Everything I'm doing here is on paper!" He believes the paperwork could be digitized if there were a desire to do so, but the bigger areas are prioritized in terms of digitalization. Arnold would really like the opportunity to do everything with his tablet. For imports, there is a digital system that enables him to finalize case processing on the spot: "It's also a good way to avoid a backlog," he says.*

*(Field notes, agricultural agency)*

In this example, frontline worker Arnold spends hours stamping and stapling piles of documents by hand while dreaming of streamlined digital solutions. Still, what stands out in our data are the situations where digitalization creates problems. This is not surprising, since we conducted our observations among frontline employees and managers who spent considerable amounts of time fixing errors and handling processes that could not be programmed (we return to the issue of programmability in Chapter 3). Our observations are therefore biased toward situations where digital technologies do not work smoothly, because these are the situations that engage the participants in our study. When things work, no human (inter)action is necessary. It is thus important to acknowledge that successful digitalization efforts *are* plentiful in both agencies—even if they mostly go unnoticed by frontline employees and managers as well as by fieldworkers and the public.

Second, it is also worth noting that participants in our study are mostly positive toward digitalization and generally wish for more and better digital technologies, although some also expressed more nostalgic sentiments. For example, Arnold's older colleague Sean, who has been with the agency for decades, explained that digitalized procedures have created a lot of extra work and made tasks more complicated for inspectors compared to "the old days." With the introduction of digital case management systems, he is now required to complete all steps in a case rather than merely handing over his handwritten inspection notes to an office clerk for further processing. This also means that he can no longer "pass the monkey along," as he sometimes used to do, but needs to resolve any problems himself. However, he notes, the requirement to follow cases through has also made the work more exciting.

With these contextual observations in mind, we now turn our attention to the question of what division of labor looks like in the digitalized bureaucracy today.

### 2.1.1  *Division of Labor Between Humans and Systems: Working the In-Between*

**Setting the alarm**

*Catherine, an experienced tax worker, has to do a number of tasks manually in the system, transferring data from one system to another. "I cannot access… oh, here we go!" she says as the system opens. She tells me that there have been reports of errors over the last few days, "and it is still a bit lazy," she says. I ask how she knows when there are errors, and she says she signed up for an email a long time ago. One of the things she needs to address is someone who has not used the*

> *proper form on the website but sent information through the old form that they used to use. "She has probably had problems with the system," Catherine concludes and corrects the numbers in the system. She then sets an alarm for herself for the next day; data is transferred between systems during the night, so she has to enter the system tomorrow to make the final corrections.*
>
> *(Field notes, tax agency)*

Examples of how systems define the work of employees abound in our material. Indeed, much of the work we have observed appears to be defined by what the systems cannot do. In "Setting the alarm," Catherine needs to enter data into the system on behalf of a company representative who for some reason failed to use the self-service system. However, because of the way the system is set up, she cannot complete the entire task at once but needs to wait until after this data has been transferred to another system, a process that happens overnight. Catherine sets an alarm on her mobile phone, as the system is not able to send reminders.

This example is one illustration of how employees spend time connecting data sources and compensating for flaws in the system—or citizens' or companies' failures to use it—as well as how the temporal structure of the digital systems (e.g., overnight data transfers) paces and determines their workflow. The need for workarounds and temporal flexibility around digital systems is also observable in "That is some workaround!".

> **That is some workaround!**
>
> *"Well, it is time for a coffee break!" says Marty. As he is getting up, a female co-worker walks over to us with her tablet in hand. "Can I ask, even though you are not a super user [i.e., a designated expert in a particular system or tool]: Have you encountered this, that it [the software] won't synchronize photos?" She explains that she has a huge forest inspection case, and now the system will not synchronize her photos; "I would be really upset to lose 29 photos!" she says. "Harriet says hers didn't work for three months, she told me this. She ended*

> up taking screenshots of all the photos and emailing them to herself." "That is some workaround!" Marty replies.
> His co-worker says she heard that if you uninstall and reinstall the system, then you lose everything. "There is no backup, is there?" she asks. "No," says Marty, "it's a closed system." They continue to discuss how the agency promised that the system would be "operationally stable" They both laugh out loud: as if! The woman says she might develop a new routine, to just double-take the photos with her mobile phone, to make sure that she has a backup.
> There is a queue at the coffee machine, so they continue their talk. The co-worker explains that the system now contains over 2,000 photos from inspections. "So definitely don't press 'Show all images'!" she says, "then things go completely wrong!" "Then it blows up!" Marty says. She explains that instead you need to zoom in until the screen shows only the section of the map that you need to use. Then you need to cut out that section and copy it into Power Point, where you then create the actual report. Marty looks at her as she explains the routine. "Shut up!?" he says loudly in an incredulous tone: "That is really stupid!". He continues to express his disbelief and then asks: "Why do you even have to take the photos in that system?" She explains that it is because "they" [i.e. higher-ups/the audit office] want them to be geo-tagged. Marty comments that the geo-tagging disappears anyway when you copy-paste it into Power Point. "That is really where you lose me completely!" The co-worker continues to explain the workaround process in detail. Marty continues to listen and comment with an expression of disbelief. His co-worker sends him a half-smile and says: "You just have to not think about it."
>
> (Field notes, agricultural agency)

Central in this example is the fact that the software used by employees is supposed to have specific properties. For example, if photos taken during inspections are not geo-referenced, this opens the possibility for fraud. Hence, the software used by inspectors must have this feature, even if it does not work well. Furthermore, while pictures need to be geo-referenced in the system when cases are forwarded internally, the workaround that employees use to manage the problems created by unintegrated software means that reports eventually do not include this information anyway—a situation that clearly frustrates employees.

As these examples illustrate, case processing often requires different types of software to be used together; but as these are often not integrated, frontline workers must "tie" them together. Frontline workers' tasks also encompass more basic operations such as waiting for updates, rebooting Wi-Fi connections, or locating required hardware such as GPS antennas. In other cases, frontline workers clean up "messes" created by digital case processing. "Clean-up duty" is an example of this. Martha tells us that all 50–60 people in her unit work on correcting mistakes generated by the automated case processing system. She emphasizes that the system mostly works well—thousands of cases are processed without problems. But in some instances, the automated processing generates new tasks for her and her co-workers. If everything were processed correctly all the time, there would be no need for their labor.

> **Clean-up duty**
>
> *Martha explains some of her tasks. When international companies pay taxes, they don't always report their CVR number. When they don't do that, their payment goes into the wrong account. Martha and her colleagues then have to place the money in the right account. To figure out where the payment comes from and where it should be placed can sometimes take up to six months. However, in that time, the system carries out all the regular automated actions like sending reminders, calculating and adding interest to unpaid debts, etc. Consequently, once Martha or one of her co-workers have figured out where the money should go, the task has multiplied: It is not simply about moving the money to the right account—they also need to backtrack all the automated steps to ensure that no company ends up paying more or less than they should, and that everything ends up registered correctly in the system. On a different occasion, another employee explains that this goes for all tasks: Everything must be accurate, as even the smallest error may be reproduced in future automated processes and lead to multiple additional errors.*
>
> *(Field notes, tax agency)*

Notably, errors rarely result from malfunctions in the system as such. In "Clean-up duty," the errors result from companies failing to report the correct information when they deposit money. In another case, Martha and her unit needed to deal with cases that had been processed incorrectly due to a sudden policy change following the COVID-19 pandemic. Since policy was changed overnight, there was no time to adjust the system, and thus many companies wrongfully received automatically processed notifications of failure to pay their debts on time, even though the government had decided to suspend all payments.

Interestingly, the division of labor between humans and digital systems is constantly re-negotiated. In "What constitutes a problem?" we see a glimpse of how this negotiation takes place in an online meeting between frontline workers and process owners, i.e., higher-level civil servants who are formally responsible for a given digitalized case process.

As Martha and Jack explain their concerns to the process owners in "What constitutes a problem?", they argue that they may be able to compensate manually for errors in the automated case processing of less complicated cases; however, as matters get more complicated, there is an increasing risk that their attempts to correct errors will end up introducing new mistakes into the system, which will then generate even more errors. On the one hand, then, automatization may lead to errors, because the system continues to process cases (i.e., payments) even if they are registered incorrectly (e.g., in the wrong account) or if policy has changed. On the other hand, attempts to fix such errors manually involve the risk of introducing new errors—a risk that increases as cases become more complex. Hence, making decisions about whether and how workers should "intervene" is not easy.

> **What constitutes a problem?**
>
> *Martha and Jack are in an online meeting with the process owners from the Copenhagen office. The meeting is a follow-up on a previous meeting. Martha and Jack discussed their strategy earlier in the day; last time they did not get the answers they wanted. The process owners are aware that they were not completely satisfied in the last meeting, so now they meet again.*

The issue is a type of case involving companies that do not have a CVR number and make payments into the wrong account. Since the postings on this account must be handled manually, it can take up to six months for employees to place the payment into the right account. During that time, companies may face reminders and accrue interest on their outstanding debts.

Jack and Martha have prepared examples and decided to start with the simplest one and gradually increase complexity. They explain how some companies received a letter to appear at a hearing, while others have been visited by the bailiff. The system pays oldest debt first, so when companies make new deposits, it may be used to pay old debt, which is actually wrongfully registered. Even when the sums are corrected, the system retains a note that the company has had outstanding debts. The process owner intervenes and says that, as long as it is not a problem for the company to have this note on their file, they should not do a lot of work to correct it.

Jack moves on to the next case. It is more complicated, and he and Martha raise concerns that they will make mistakes when they have to handle it manually. For larger companies, many changes are needed, which increases the risk of mistakes. The process owner adds: "Maybe this is just one of these things that we cannot really solve?" Jack responds: "We have another example, it gets a lot worse!" The process owner says: "So essentially you think that this process of backtracking and removing interest and payments is going to be too messy?" "Yes, but we should do it anyway," Jack says.

Martha intervenes. She does not understand the answer from the lawyers that they had previously obtained. It is, after all, the companies who have made the mistakes, and now they want to treat them better than other companies, who also make mistakes? On the other hand, she later states, if payments come from a particular bank, they might have added their CVR number, but it disappears in the transfer. Sometimes, the companies can document that they have done all the right things, and it still looks wrong in the system.

They move on to the next case and go through the details. The process owner intervenes: "I don't think we need to change that—that is way too big a task." He continues: "Let's not blow this out of proportion." Jack continues his explanation and Martha adds: "But then we treat

> *them better, because they made a mistake." She suggests they make it even more clear on the website that they need to include their CVR.*
>
> *The process owner announces: "I have another meeting in 2 minutes," but acknowledges that they have not found a solution yet and need to involve the legal experts: "What I hear you say is that this does not work in practice." They talk about the practical implications, e.g. that the bailiff may go out to collect wrongful debts, and the process owner ends by stating that the legal department "often makes decisions where they do not consider the operational level, but that is why we are here." He says they will go another round with the legal department and asks Jack and Martha to forward the examples to them, so that they can pass them on. They sum up the meeting and say goodbye.*
>
> *(Field notes, tax agency)*

Overall, we find that digital technologies enable the handling of large caseloads, allowing humans to focus on critical cases and supporting a functional division of labor. At the same time, digital technologies can complicate the clear division of labor between humans and systems because boundaries are constantly re-negotiated between tasks that are done by humans and those that are handled inside digital systems.

The examples in this section illustrate that frontline workers are indispensable in terms of carrying out necessary manual operations to compensate for flaws and correct errors, and that, in doing so, they are uniquely positioned to notice the risks involved as well as inconsistencies in higher-level decision-making. As the example further illustrates, negotiations and clarifications concerning which tasks employees can reasonably be asked to take on, and hence the division of labor between humans and digital systems, take place among a number of organizational actors, including process owners, the legal department, and IT developers. In these negotiations, participants struggle to gain a sufficient overview and understanding of how things work outside of their own unit, and this lack of overview and insight clearly complicates decision-making. This leads us to further examine the division of labor between the operative core and the IT organization.

### 2.1.2 Division of Labor Between the Operative Core and the IT Organization: Bridging the Gaps

While our observations focus on frontline managers and employees, we are constantly reminded that to make the digitalized bureaucracy work, IT professionals and legal specialists also need to be involved. As "Construction site meeting" illustrates, the ongoing work of ensuring both efficient processes and legality is played out in a complicated relationship between frontline workers (system users), process owners, and IT specialists.

> **Construction site meeting**
>
> *Keith brings me along to a construction site meeting. The meeting includes 11 participants, including process owners, system owners, and the ones using the systems, i.e., Keith and his employees. The process owners are three younger men, situated in the same office in a different part of the country.*
>
> *They start out by updating on some tests they are running. Moving along what seems to be a pre-set agenda, the process owners realize that a certain task is done manually in the unit. One of the process owners is surprised: "Hold on, that is news to me!" he exclaims. The discussion moves back and forth, trying to establish agreement as to why these things cannot be done in the system. If it can be done centrally, it seems very wasteful to have people doing it. Keith's employees do their best to explain why it has been done manually, but the process owners are still surprised. "That sounds like a lot..." one of them states. Even among the employees, there seem to be different interpretations of why and how the task is done. One of them gets slightly upset: "You don't know how much work is in this!".*
>
> *One of the process owners interrupts, "Now we have heard some different perspectives," and finishes the debate by arguing that they need to consider what to do but in a different "room," i.e. in a different group of people. Keith intervenes and argues that this has been a really big job for his unit. If it can be done automatically, it is somewhat problematic that they have not been told. "The system owner needs to get involved," one of the process owners states.*

> *The debate continues; most of the amounts in question are rather small, "but we still need to work in accordance with the law," as one states. They end up agreeing that more work needs to be done. "Please include me," one of Keith's employees asks. "Anyone else who needs to be involved?" the process owner asks. No one answers.*
>
> *The next item on the agenda involves some legal changes that were made due to Covid-19—and now the system cannot incorporate them. This again leads to manual work for the unit.*
>
> *Next up they discuss a service window, i.e., a time frame for software updates where systems will be inoperable. It has been announced late and now it coincides with the scheduled time where they send out reminders of outstanding debt. They go back and forth; if the service window is to be moved, someone will have to work the weekend.*
>
> *They move through a few agenda items where no one has anything to say. Finally, Keith raises an issue that was raised by his employees in a meeting the day before: the number of mouse clicks needed to do certain tasks. He points out that is has implications both for the efficiency and the well-being of employees. "We're on your team, Keith," the process owner states. "We will look into it." A few other issues are raised, and the meeting ends.*
>
> *(Field notes, tax agency)*

"Construction site meetings" are typically held during the construction of a new building or, in this case, a new digital system. However, our observations show that even if the development and testing phase has formally ended, these "construction site meetings" are often kept in place, as issues and errors continue to appear, and IT specialists and process owners depend on frontline workers' practical experience and knowledge of how things are done in order to be able to fix these errors. Legal advisors are also important actors in this setup, although they do not participate directly in discussions.

In these interactions, we see that it takes work to establish a common understanding of issues, to place responsibility for handling these issues, and sometimes even to figure out who needs to be engaged to solve problems. One explanation for this is that digitalization involves fragmentation, as different types of cases are processed in different systems, and the processing of cases within those systems is split into smaller processes, some of which are automated and hence "invisible" to those who are responsible. At the same time, digitalization also appears to entail fragmentation in relation to formal hierarchical structures and division of labor. In our observations of the construction site meetings, we did not always identify who was actually capable of making decisions about the way forward, and we often observed interactions like the one recounted above, where different perspectives were introduced, but where conclusions and authority to make decisions remained opaque.

Our observations in the agricultural agency also include examples of how digital technologies introduce uncertainty about division of labor and decision structures. In "Technical or human error?", agricultural inspector Jane recounts a process in which she and her co-workers feared that some farmers had been treated unfairly and asked for the cases to be double-checked. However, only IT specialists were able to distinguish between human and technical errors; the inspectors themselves could not make this judgment. Due to a backlog in the IT support unit and a lack of managerial involvement in the process, inspectors were left waiting for a long time until finally a decision was made that allowed them to move forward and inform the farmers that their cases would be reopened and reassessed.

> **Technical or human error?**
>
> *Like other inspectors, Jane divides her time between the regional office, her home office, and physical inspections. Today, I am sitting next to her at her desk. After a long moment of silence, she leans back and sighs. Last year, she tells me, the agency launched an app where farmers could send in geo-tagged photos of their fields within a deadline to prove compliance with regulations. They need this approval to receive subsidies. The app is an example of how the agency is seeking to transition from physical to administrative inspections in some areas.*
>
> *At first, they accepted photos via email, but the Audit Office did not approve, because the photos were not geo-tagged, and so there was no way of knowing whether they were genuine. Then they developed the app, but some farmers experienced problems. The rules state that if they miss the deadline due to a technical error, they can get a dispensation.*

> *However, only IT specialists were able to distinguish technical errors from human errors. The inspectors could not make that judgment.*
>
> *Jane says she believes some farmers may have received a rejection even though they had correctly reported a technical error. This is quite problematic, she says, because even if these cases concern only a small subsidy, a rejection means that payments of all other subsidies will be put on hold. Farmers expect and need this money for bank transfers, so the consequences can be severe. It has now been decided that they will reopen some of the cases. Inspectors have been asked to inform the farmers, because they are used to talking to the farmers. "It is not exactly a dream job," she says.*
>
> *(Field notes, agricultural agency)*

In addition to internal organizational complexity and fragmentation, the division of labor between the operating core and the IT developers also relates to the policy environment, which we touched upon earlier. Because both tax legislation and agricultural legislation tend to be adjusted frequently, digital systems must be adapted accordingly, and adaptations must be tested before they are put into practice. Some agricultural inspectors, like Jane, spend approximately three months per year on this process of testing, in which higher-level bureaucrats (process owners) serve as links to the IT developers. As illustrated in "Some of us have no prerequisites," this task can leave frontline workers feeling somewhat lost.

> **Some of us have no prerequisites**
>
> *Jane logs on to the online meeting and introduces me to the other participants. They joke and check whether everyone is present. The process owner opens the meeting and begins by asking everyone to reflect on last year's testing process—not the individual cases, but the process as such? Jane volunteers to begin. "It was very messy," she says, "...difficult to get into, I did not know if I knew what I needed to know, you know? I had some cases waiting for a long time. Finally, towards the end, someone told me that I could just do so-and-so. But that feeling*

> of, am I doing something wrong or is it actually an error? It feels a bit much to reach out to [the responsible higher-level bureaucrat] if it is just me." (...).
> Later in the meeting, another participant recounts a presentation last year that left her completely bewildered. It was about what was new since last time, and "we did not understand a thing." "I was so frustrated; I hate not to understand or know." The presentation only lasted 1½ hours, "but it felt like nine," she says. This year, it would be good to take it from scratch so that everyone can follow.
> Jane says she agrees. Consider the fact that many testers will be new, she says. "Also, when you send out an email: "We are switching dates," what does that mean? Include a couple of sentences to explain (...). Think about the fact that some of us have no prerequisites for understanding."
>
> (Field notes, agricultural agency)

In this case, Jane feels like she does not have the sufficient knowledge or understanding of the digital system or the process of testing to do what the process owners and IT developers need. She explains how she mistrusts her own judgment ("am I doing something wrong or is it actually an error?") and she feels uncertain about reaching out for support if it is "just her." In other instances, process owners and other higher-ups were less knowledgeable than frontline workers about how things were done and hence highly dependent on their insights. We see this in "Construction site meeting." "Lost in organization" also illustrates this. This example further illustrates how the complicated nature of the organization makes it difficult even for experienced employees to navigate and locate formal authority.

> **Lost in organization**
>
> Catherine has been with the tax agency for 15 years. Her expression is kind but strict, like a seasoned schoolteacher, and her desk and surroundings are neat: no decorations, and no mess. On day three, she reveals a tiny pile of clutter, including a cardboard calendar, neatly

> *tucked away under her desk mat. The day before, on my second day in the tax agency, she told me about an upcoming meeting that she is excited about.*
>
> *The meeting is about calculation of interest, mistakes made in the past, and expiration dates. It has so far been unclear how they should deal with this, and they have yet to receive an answer. Catherine explains that she disagrees with Ryan on how to deal with expired cases according to the law. Ryan is the process owner, a higher-level bureaucrat, and he is responsible for clarifying the situation. She tells me that Ryan is new to this role and does not know much about this type of case: "He has been thrown into a bunch of things that he needs to figure out," Catherine says.*
>
> *I ask where he is formally located in the organization, if she could show me? That is a good question, Catherine says. She turns to her screen, finds the intranet, and scrolls down a page with the title "Newly Employed." She then looks at a diagram showing all seven agencies in the ministry. She clicks on various links and boxes. She then finds another site and clicks on "pre- and onboarding." Finally, she locates the agency's organizational diagram. She clicks to enlarge it and looks at it for a while. She is not sure which unit Ryan belongs to. She searches for an email to see what his auto signature says, but his emails do not have one. I briefly notice the content in one of them. It is a short response to Catherine. The text reads: "You are right; I am mixing up the two legislations," followed by several smileys.*
>
> (Field notes, tax agency)

In many of the interactions we have witnessed and illustrated so far, the consequences for citizens and the obligation to ensure that they are treated fairly and equally take center stage. In "What constitutes a problem?", we see that Martha is deeply concerned about the consequences of higher-level decisions and raises this point several times during the meeting. Likewise, in "Technical or human error?", Jane and her co-workers act on their concern that some farmers might have been treated unfairly due to technical errors, which leads to a cumbersome process of reopening and reassessing several cases, including the unpleasant task of having to call all the farmers to let them know. At the same time, however, the fact that much of this case processing happens "inside" the digital systems makes it difficult for frontline workers or others to detect problems and act on their concerns, just as it is sometimes difficult to distinguish between technical and human errors or even to determine *if* something is an error. As illustrated in "Technically, there is nothing wrong," cases may be processed digitally as intended, and still the outcome can be wrong.

> **Technically, there is nothing wrong**
>
> *Keith is a frontline manager in the tax agency. Every morning, his unit gathers for a meeting to share important information and do "the round." The round is a process where all employees take turns telling their co-workers which tasks they will be working on today. This is also an opportunity to ask questions if they have any doubts or ask for assistance on specific tasks, e.g., due to pressing deadlines. This morning, we are halfway through the round when one of the younger employees explains a problematic batch of cases. He explains that a reminder was automatically sent out in October. Many businesses were informed that they had unpaid debts when in fact they had already paid. The automated case processing system had "eaten them [i.e., processed their payments] in the wrong order." Another co-worker interrupts: "The wrong order? No, it is the right order!" "Yes," says the first speaker, "technically there is nothing wrong," but, he explains, the deadlines for some payments were extended due to the COVID-19 lockdown, yet this adjustment had not been programmed in the system. And so, given this rapid policy change, the automated processing of the businesses' payments was actually wrong.*
>
> *(Field notes, tax agency)*

There also seems to be a continual balancing between what is considered efficient and legitimate from an organizational perspective, e.g., the minimum amount that should be collected or paid out, and the demand for legality. "What is acceptable?" illustrates this from the viewpoint of managers. Systems call for accuracy, which is desired, but often time is spent on tasks with very limited revenue, as the amounts in question may indeed be very small (i.e., cents). This leads to discussions about administrative efficiency versus accuracy as well as consistency and equal treatment. In this example, managers highlight the interests of stakeholders, who should not be left worse off in this balancing act.

> **What is acceptable?**
>
> *During a meeting, managers from different units are discussing to what extent they are able to handle refunds for companies. They discuss how different technical solutions allow them to process refunds, and what should be the lower limit for refunds. It becomes obvious from the conversation that there is not one standard and that systems do not support a uniform effort. "My employees are frustrated," one manager exclaims. "It is embarrassing when corrections are too small," another adds. In the following debate, they discuss the extent to which they identify all relevant cases and agree that they probably do not. Someone has started changing procedures, because they had gotten the idea that this was how everyone was doing it—"but that would take 11 FTE," [i.e., Full Time Equivalents] one of the managers states. They obviously do not do it. "That is not defensible from an administrative point of view," one adds, and they agree that employees should not send out emails about the guidelines. "This is crazy," one mutters; "But at least we are not putting the companies in a worse position than before," another one adds.*
>
> *(Field notes, tax agency)*

Notably, a second layer of concerns is also raised in "What is acceptable?" There are obvious trade-offs between revenue generated, legality, and organizational capacity. Digital systems allow for certain tasks, including corrections, to be carried out "cheaply," whereas others are much more demanding for the organization if they have to be done manually. The "organizational price" may not be related to revenue impact or legality at all but is still an important component when priorities are determined.

Summing up, when studying division of labor between the operative core and the IT organization, we find that the pervasiveness of digital technologies increases the complexity and fragmentation of the organization. Sometimes, this results in blurred lines of responsibility and

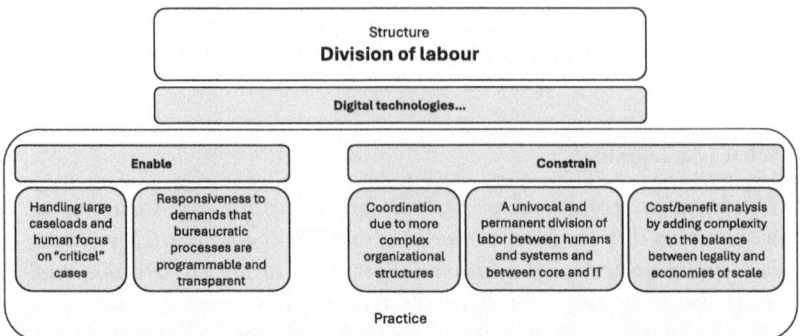

Fig. 2.1 How digital technologies enable and constrain division of labor

lacunae of authority in negotiations of the division of labor around digital technologies. Finally, we find that digital technologies add a layer of complexity in determining what should be handled by humans, what should be programmed into systems, and what should be left alone. Beyond criteria such as revenue (economies of scale) and legality (equal treatment of citizens), we also identify concerns regarding the complexity of systems and the cost of development/the risk of human errors in highly digitalized processes. These findings are summarized in Fig. 2.1.

## 2.2 Hierarchy in the Digitalized Bureaucracy

We now turn to the second central feature: hierarchy. We begin by examining what managers actually do in the digitalized bureaucracy. Our observations show how the position of the manager is not necessarily tied to superior expertise; rather, we see frontline managers acting as facilitators in different ways and we find that this is often tightly linked to the digitalized nature of the organization.

### 2.2.1 What Managers Do in the Digitalized Bureaucracy

The basic idea of hierarchical organizing rests on the assumption that managers make more complicated decisions as they move up the hierarchy. However, when observing frontline managers and employees in highly digitalized organizations, we find that frontline managers spend a lot of time on facilitating the work of their employees: They turn the power back on when blackouts happen, check whether their employees have access to Wi-Fi and what kind of equipment they need at their work stations. They order headsets and monitors and keyboards and are generally involved in ensuring that the physical and material aspects of digitalized work are in place. In a sense, frontline managers behave almost as secretaries as they focus on the practical issues around employees' use of digital systems and constantly seek to fix issues as they arise. This perspective is underscored in "A black hole." In addition to highlighting the earlier point regarding division of labor between employees and IT specialists, this example illustrates how frontline managers experience their own role in this: To speak on behalf of employees who are more knowledgeable than they are.

> **A black hole**
>
> *I ask Keith why Jessica participated in the construction site meeting. He tells me that she was part of an "error detection group" that existed for 10 years. She has a strong network and therefore it is good to include her in these conversations. His own role is to "advance issues" that are important to his employees. In relation to operations, his employees are more knowledgeable, whereas his perspective is more general.*
>
> *He explains that there used to be only two process owners. One would seldom get a reply if one tried to raise an issue. It was like a "black hole," he says, and it resulted in anarchy. Everyone would come up with different workarounds when systems failed, because they could not get help in any other way. Today there are nine process owners, and they take the construction site meetings much more seriously. Still, meetings are prioritized below other pressing issues. They used to meet in person, but now they only meet online. Keith says it is not the same—you do not build the same kind of network. It would be good if they could meet in person 2–3 times per year.*
>
> *(Field notes, tax agency)*

Notably, much of the work of frontline managers is intrinsically linked to administering and facilitating access to software as well as hardware. The main focus of these activities is to ensure that frontline workers can do their jobs, and nothing more. In other words, controlling and restricting access is equally important. Rather than fulfilling the role of supervisors whose authority rests on superior expertise, frontline managers act as "digital gatekeepers." On our first day in the tax agency, frontline manager Beatrice spent a large part of the day trying to ensure access for new employees, as illustrated in "Only managers."

> **Only managers**
>
> *Today, Beatrice welcomes three new employees in her unit. However, it quickly turns out that the new employees cannot access the IT systems. Beatrice calls the support line; the wait is long. While she is on hold, she talks to the new employees about how to adjust their screens. Finally, her call goes through and she explains the issue to the helpdesk. Another new employee points out that she received a different message regarding the password. While helpdesk is on the phone, a new employee tests whether the internet cable fits her laptop; it does not.*
>
> *Beatrice puts the woman from the helpdesk on speaker and walks into the open plan office, asking the new employee to try the new password, following instructions from the helpdesk officer. The software prompts the employee to make a new code, but employees cannot do that by themselves. Then the computer just stops: "It's just idling," Beatrice says to the woman on the phone. It's the same for all new employees.*
>
> *Beatrice and the new employee try several different things while on the phone with the helpdesk: another laptop, laptop in docking station, the new employee entering the wrong password three times, "Is caps lock on?" They continue to try to figure out what is wrong. Another call illuminates Beatrice's phone—she ignores it and stays on the call with helpdesk. According to the helpdesk, one employee has entered the password wrong six times. "But I was next to him, I saw what he did, he did not write the wrong password six times!" says Beatrice. Helpdesk suggests getting a second opinion. "She is gone, she did not hang up!" Beatrice is visibly distraught when the connection is cut off.*
>
> *Beatrice calls back, the phone rings, no one picks up. She has to call the main number again and go through the screening again. She knows the drill and pushes the numbers before she hears the instructions. An automated message tells her that "only managers can order log-ins for new employees"—Beatrice knows and mutters in an ironic*

> *voice:* "*This makes so much sense—that I have to spend my time on this.*" *Finally, the woman from the helpdesk calls back.*
>
> *(Field notes, tax agency)*

This example illustrates how the issue of access becomes a priority when welcoming new employees, and how a lack of access is problematic to the extent that the manager ends up spending hours trying to fix it. Notably, they cannot delegate this task, because only they have the authority to administer access. Gaining access, however, is not just a problem for new employees. Seasoned employees also often experience problems when having to engage with new systems or systems that they do not frequently use, as illustrated in "Not authorized." Managers consequently spend considerable time and energy facilitating and regulating employees' access to systems.

> **Not authorized**
>
> *Marianne has been banned from a software that she does not use much. She has never tried being banned before. "Too many failed attempts to log in," she explains to me while she checks the chat. "I have to call the helpdesk." She navigates through the screening and gets a person on the phone. She states her user number and explains her issue: "Someone from IT said that I am not authorized," she explains. However, after a few seconds, she has access. A co-worker chimes in: The problem with access to systems often happens when people change jobs within the organization. "It works just fine for Harriet," who is new to the agency.*
>
> *(Field notes, tax agency)*

Keeping track of who is granted access to which systems emerges as a central task to ensure that the authority vested in the tax authorities is used in a proper manner. As illustrated in "100% control," this is a question of control. The manager needs to be sure that employees cannot access sensitive information that they are not authorized to read and ensure that employees cannot defraud the system. Throughout our fieldwork, we encountered references to the "Britta scandal." In 2018, the Danish Authority of Social Services uncovered massive fraud by a trusted employee named Britta Nielsen. From 1993 to 2018, she stole around 117 million DKK by fraudulently transferring money reserved for social service efforts to her own accounts. The case illustrated a lack of controls governing who could transfer and approve transfers in Danish government agencies. Subsequently, the Danish Court of Auditors as well as government agencies took a close look at such practices, and this awareness is strongly reflected in our material as well; not least when it comes to who can access systems and who is allowed to transfer money and how such transfers are approved.

> **100% control**
>
> *Beatrice has a brief moment to herself. She checks her email and shows me a PowerPoint presentation: "We've been praised for this," she adds. She explains that it is important that the employees only have permissions in the systems that they currently need. It counts negatively in the internal control if employees have too many permissions. A permission allows you to change amounts and "money," and employees should be kept from "messing" with things that are not their business. For a while Beatrice has had a policy of 100% control over permissions—meaning that they had been checking all permissions. But from now on they will only do random samples. If mistakes are found, they will then have to expand the controls. But most often it is "error 40"—random mistakes.*
>
> *(Field notes, tax agency)*

Frequently, fixing problems of access requires help from support functions, as illustrated in the example regarding access above, where frontline manager Beatrice had to repeatedly call the helpdesk. In everyday practice, we frequently observed frontline workers engaging in practices of collaborative IT support as an alternative to formalized IT support, which they often experience as insufficient to meet their needs (a point also illustrated earlier in "That is some workaround!") (see also Møller 2023). However, there is no getting around the formal support when it comes to access. In

"Playing support right," we see how managers also play an important role in conveying knowledge about how to interact with IT support. Specifically, we learn that there are certain ways (not) to handle the support systems to both receive the necessary support and avoid unnecessary costs.

> **Playing support right**
>
> *Theresa has some issues with her phone—she cannot access the Wi-Fi and hence cannot access her emails on the phone. Beatrice argues that there has to be some way to make it work—"but don't call the IT support," she says. She recommends that Theresa makes a case in the system, and then she will get in touch with someone who can actually help—as opposed to the person you will get on the phone. "But do not order a new phone," Beatrice emphasizes. "Ask for a return, then we do not have to pay again."*
>
> *(Field notes, tax agency)*

Further, as illustrated in "It just has to work," it is not uncommon for frontline managers to become deeply involved in interactions with IT support on behalf of employees in relation to other types of issues, for example when case management systems crash. If the systems do not function, employees cannot perform inspections in the field or process cases in the office. Malfunctioning systems therefore become a top priority for frontline managers, even if there is little they can do on their own, as the examples also illustrate.

> **It just has to work!**
>
> *Robert, a manager, sits next to John, who tries to access a particular software on his computer. This was also an issue yesterday. Another employee comes by, says she had an issue with the software as well yesterday, then moves on. Robert opens a case with IT support, then gets a number of different error codes that they do not understand. It is not the first time, and it is "highly frustrating," but if the system does*

> *not work, they cannot make their reports. When asked what constitutes the problem, the employee says "Robert knows"—but he clearly indicates that he doesn't, and that it is the helpdesk that needs to fix it.*
>
> *Robert goes on to ask about the inspections they have to carry out today. They can still make it on time, and they can do the inspection without the software. "It just has to work!" the employee states. "Okay, this was the first one." Robert goes on to the next problem that has to be reported. They try to open another software program, but it just loads and loads. "Not responding," the employee reads from the screen; that is the problem. The software does not open. They discuss workarounds, but still file a report and discuss how to frame the problem in the report. "Then we have done something," says the employee. Robert follows up, stating that they should probably have a reply in a few days, maybe sooner if others complain as well. "You can also call them." To me he says that sometimes they do not report and just hope things fix themselves. But they agree that they should report.*
>
> *(Field notes, agricultural agency)*

We have so far focused on access to software. However, as noted above, managers are also focused on physical and material aspects of work. Indeed, there is also a material side to the issue of access. "Missing antennae" illustrates the work that agricultural agency frontline manager Robert carries out to ensure that employees have access to the hardware they need to carry out their jobs. In this case, Robert is dealing with a problem regarding GPS antennae. The antennae are a prerequisite for several types of physical inspections that require precise measurements of, e.g., areas or distances between fields and fences. Although employees have tablets and mobile phones with similar functionality, these are not ISO certified and hence not approved by the European Union.[1] Therefore, they cannot be used, even if they are more precise than the antennae. As the agency faces an increased workload on a particular type of inspection that requires antennae, it becomes clear that there is a hardware shortage. Managers and employees agree that sharing the antennae is not

---

[1] The majority of rules and subsidies administered by the agency stem from the European Union.

a solution, as this would require employees to drive for hours to the office to pick up and return antennae before and after inspections.

Similar concerns are evident regarding the placement and accessibility of special printers or stamps needed to authorize imports and exports of plants in the agricultural agency, or the functionality of headsets in the tax agency. For example, employees observed that newly acquired headsets allowed their colleagues in the open office space to listen in when citizens called in for advice. As the headsets did not sufficiently close off citizens' voices, there was a risk that citizens would unwillingly and unknowingly share private and sensitive information with a broader audience. In this way, hardware also becomes a primary concern for frontline managers.

> **Missing antennae**
>
> *Later in the day, Robert calls the company that provides antennae. He asks whether they have any used antennae they could sell the agency? The woman on the other end of the line says that she will get someone to call him back. He also wants to check up on an antenna that has been in for repair. He provides a number, and the woman makes a note. Robert later tells me that the antennae are essential for the agency to do the inspections they have been asked to do, and they are in short supply all over the world. Robert has been googling where to buy these antennae and has been in contact with several suppliers. He even found some in Singapore, but there are security concerns with such a purchase. So now they try to have them repaired.*
>
> *(Field notes, agricultural agency)*

Finally, managers also spend a lot of time handling their email. In an organization where many things are programmed (cf. Chapter 3), email is a highly unstructured digital technology that allows for many different purposes and uses. It also contributes greatly to the complexity of everyday life, as email allows for an unlimited inflow of unsorted information and requests on a timeline controlled by the sender, not the recipient.

Our fieldwork data abundantly demonstrates that emails are a constant in the lives of the managers, who struggle to keep them "down." Most notably, emails significantly increase the number of issues on which a manager can be kept informed. Some emails are an essential cog in the larger wheel of the organization—for example when managers need to approve claims and entries over certain amounts—but email is also used to inform recipients about the latest changes to the plan for the Christmas party, potential criticism from the Danish court of auditors, new guidelines, and a number of other issues, some of major and others of minor importance.

In "Information overload," we see how one manager tries to discipline his relationship with his email. Peter's experience is closely mirrored in many of our observations of managers who all spend a large amount of time answering and reading emails and employed different strategies for controlling this permanent stream of information. For example, frontline manager Beatrice had a designated folder for issues that needed her attention and follow-up. At the time of observation, it contained 85 emails. This was not unusual.

> **Information overload**
>
> *Peter, a manager, has a break from meetings and picks up his phone to read emails—he has shut down the email notifications on the phone, because he wants to stay in charge. If you are "on" all the time, it will wear you down, he explains. He knows that not paying attention all the time may lead him to miss the opportunity to weigh in on things, but then he is also not responsible. Often, he is just in cc on emails, or others solve issues without him. He tries to systematize his emails by having different folders: one for issues that need approval, one for new rules, etc. If he must do something, he marks the email as unread. Emails take up a lot of his time. "It's like tennis—you have to return and keep it down," he says.*
>
> *(Field notes, tax agency)*

In "Information overload," Peter makes a point of turning of email notifications to regain at least some control. However, we generally observed managers checking and answering emails at any given moment during the day, including during both physical and virtual meetings that

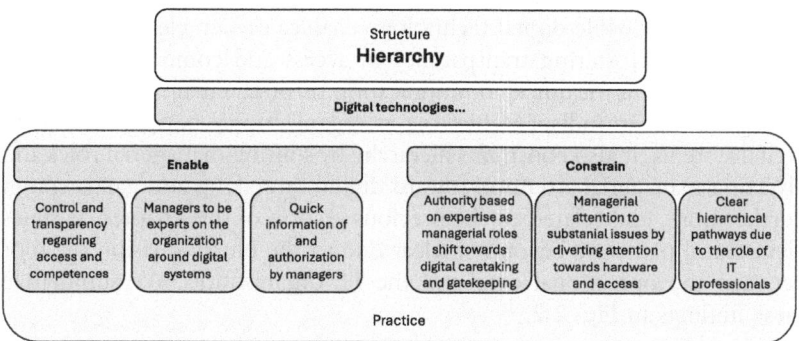

**Fig. 2.2** How digital technologies enable and constrain hierarchy

required their attention. Quite often, however, the manger does not need to "do" anything about the emails they read; they just need to be informed—a "cc culture," as it is described in one of the agencies. In the digitalized bureaucracy, emails have multiple functions and purposes, including as instruments for accountability because they allow actors to document that information has been shared and consent has been given. Hence they become an important mediator in the relationship between employees and managers in terms of accountability and authorization.

Overall, we find that managers carry out a great number of tasks that, on the surface, may seem trivial, relating to employees' access to systems and hardware. However, we also see that some of these seemingly trivial tasks are less so when understood in a bureaucratic logic: While it may seem trivial to call the helpdesk to obtain system permissions, system access plays an essential role in ensuring the privacy of citizens and the proper handling of their sensitive data and, not least, in controlling employees' access to public funds. The question of authorization and access hence becomes a key ingredient in organizing a digitalized bureaucracy. Decision-making competences follow formalized hierarchical structures but also depend on access to systems and the ability to allow others to access these systems. With access comes responsibility and accountability. Further, we see that issues related to, e.g., efficiency and information security in digitalized case processing are strongly intertwined with the physical and material world. Hardware is just as important as software, and frontline managers spend much of their time attending to both.

We find that while digital technology enables certain elements of hierarchy, e.g., by fostering transparency in access and competences within systems, allowing for quick communication through email, and providing managers with an indispensable role as organizational navigators around digital systems, it also constrains hierarchy by shifting managerial roles and diverting managerial attention toward digital caretaking and gatekeeping. Furthermore, and related to the previous section of this chapter, at times hierarchical pathways become unclear due to the blurry division of labor between the operational core and the IT organization. We summarize these findings in Fig. 2.2.

## References

Durkheim, Émile. 2008. *The Division of Labor in Society*. 13. [Repr.]. New York: Free Press.
Foss, Nicolai J., and Peter G. Klein. 2014. Why Managers Still Matter. *MIT Sloan Management Review* 56 (1): 73–80.
Freudenburg, William R. 1993. Risk and Recreancy: Weber, the Division of Labor, and the Rationality of Risk Perceptions. *Social Forces* 71 (4): 909. https://doi.org/10.2307/2580124.
Galbraith, Jay R. 1977. *Organization Design*. Reading, MA: Addison-Wesley Pub. Co.
Gulick, Luther. 1937. "Notes on the Theory of Organization" in: Luther Gulick and Lyndall Urwick. *Papers on the Science of Administration*, Institute of Public Administration, New York, NY: Columbia University, 1–36.
March, James Gardner, and Herbert Alexander Simon. 1993. *Organizations*, 2nd ed. New York: John Wiley & Sons.
Møller, Anne Mette. 2023. "Inside the Digital State: Frontline Workers and Digital Transformation of Government." Paper presented at the *Public Management Research Conference (PMRC)*, Utrecht University, The Netherlands, June 27–30.
Simon, Herbert A. 1982. *Models of Bounded Rationality*. Cambridge, MA: MIT Press.
Weber, Max. 1978. *Economy and Society: An Outline of Interpretive Sociology*. Edited by G. Roth and C. Wittich. Berkeley: University of California Press.
Weber, Max. 1997. *Makt og byråkrati: essays om politikk og klasse, samfunnsforskning og verdier*. 2. utg., 5. oppl. Oslo: Gyldendal.

CHAPTER 3

# Rules, Programmability, and Discretion in the Digitalized Bureaucracy

**Abstract** This chapter focuses on the rational-legal authority associated with public bureaucracies, namely legality and the rule of law. In the *Rechtsstaat*, where the rule of law prevails, citizens should be able to know which rules apply, how they will be applied, and what to expect. We understand rules as generalized principles for decision-making that are applicable within a defined area, and which can be applied to individual cases. The chapter shows how digital technologies interact with rules, programmability, and frontline workers' exercise of discretion. The chapter discusses how this affects the bureaucratic ethos of employees and bureaucratic values such as transparency and responsiveness.

**Keywords** Bureaucracy · Rules · Programmability · Discretion · Public encounter · Citizens · Transparency · Responsiveness · Bureaucratic ethos

In Chapter 2, we presented our empirical analysis of how digitalization shapes the daily work of frontline employees and managers and discussed how digital technologies influence division of labor and traditional hierarchies in the two agencies. In this chapter, we turn our attention to a third and equally central feature of the rational-legal authority associated with public bureaucracies, namely legality and the rule of law. More specifically, we focus on rules, programmability, and frontline workers' exercise of discretion in the digitalized bureaucracy.

Rules are at the center of the bureaucratic model. We understand rules as generalized principles for decision-making that are applicable within a defined area, and which can be applied to individual cases. We furthermore expect rules to be relatively durable and hence create predictability for citizens (Jespersen 1996). In the *Rechtsstaat*, where the rule of law prevails, citizens should be able to know which rules apply, how they will be applied, and what to expect (Bovens and Zouridis 2002).

However, rules can also be understood as representing and reifying institutions. As Olsen (2006, 9) points out, "rules provide codes of meaning that facilitate the interpretation of ambiguous worlds. They embody collective and individual roles, identities, rights, obligations, interests, values, worldviews, and memory and thus constrain the allocation of attention, standards of evaluation, priorities, perceptions, and resources." Hence, rules in the abstract are part of what constitutes social structure and defines roles and identities in public bureaucracies. We therefore expect that a breach of rules not only has implications for the integrity of the rules in question but also has wider implications for employees' bureaucratic ethos.

Empirically, rules may come directly from the legal basis on which agencies are founded but may also be more local. Often, rules are reflected in guidelines, formalized best practices, or similar "translations" from abstract legal documents into everyday practices. In our data, we are interested in rule-based and "programmed" behavior, i.e., situations where behavior is regulated by guidelines, instructions, handbooks, codes of conduct, or similar artifacts that clarify, sometimes in great detail, how employees should handle different tasks. We take this as an outset for discussing the extent to which human behavior in the digitalized bureaucracies appears as programmed and programmable, similar to what is done when tasks are automated in digital systems.

Importantly, while the bureaucratic organization entails standardization and predictability, bureaucrats are also required to exercise discretion. In organization theory, discretion is typically viewed as the room for maneuver that is needed to make organizations run. If all instances of uncertainty are relayed to a superior, organizations will suffer from overload at the top levels of the hierarchy (Galbraith 1977). In the literature on public policy and public administration, debates over discretion often focus on bureaucratic discretion and its consequences for policy implementation. It is a well-established fact that legislation is sometimes ambiguous "on purpose" (e.g., McCubbins, Noll and Weingast 1987), to ease compromise among stakeholders or because it is too difficult for policymakers to foresee how legislation could be made less ambiguous in complex environments. Despite the rule-based nature of public bureaucracies, much decision-making in practice relies on the discretion of public servants. These perspectives highlight the importance of bureaucratic expertise to ensure organizational efficiency and competent decision-making. This is also a central tenet of Weberian bureaucracy (Møller, Pedersen and Pors 2022).

However, the discretionary powers of frontline workers are often considered a double-edged sword. While ambiguity and complexity should ideally be referred to higher organizational echelons (cf. Chapter 2), employees at lower organizational levels, i.e., street-level bureaucrats, are often left to deal with ambiguous rules and complexity in practice (Lipsky 2010; Zacka 2017). While scholars acknowledge that street-level discretion is necessary (e.g., to ensure equal treatment by taking particular circumstances into account in the assessment of individual cases), it introduces a risk of arbitrariness, as street-level bureaucrats "continuously make decisions, major and minor, about whether or not to apply the rules and how they should be interpreted in a specific case" (Bovens and Zouridis 2002, 175).

According to Bovens and Zouridis, digitalization significantly reduces the scope of administrative discretion at the street level, as client data must be registered in fixed templates in electronic forms, most decisions are programmed into software design and digital decision trees, and employees are constantly connected to the organization via digital devices that register every action they take. Instead, discretionary powers reside with software developers and IT professionals. Our analysis in Chapter 2 supports this idea to some extent, but also underscores that, even in the "system-level bureaucracy," frontline workers still play indispensable roles. Digitalization does not make street-level discretion disappear, but it shifts its nature (Buffat 2015; Busch & Henriksen 2018; Marienfeldt 2024).

Notably, Bovens and Zouridis also suggest that, while digital technologies "make it possible to perfect the legality of the execution in the extreme" by diminishing or eliminating street-level discretion, there is a risk that the rigidity of digitalized decision-making will introduce a different kind of arbitrariness, as "[c]omputerization, taken too far, makes insufficient allowance for special circumstances and can lead to absurd or downright hazardous situations" (Bovens and Zouridis 2002, 182). Our examples in Chapter 2 also highlight this risk.

In the following, we examine how rules, programmability, discretion, and digital technologies interact in the two agencies in our study.

## 3.1 Rules and Programmability in the Digitalized Bureaucracy

As noted in Chapter 2, participants in our study often express their satisfaction with the fact that many tasks and processes have been digitalized or even automated. In "Most of it runs really well," Martha takes care to explain that, while some automated processes generate work for her and her co-workers in the form of errors that must be corrected, most automated processes function as intended. Clearly, there are considerable efficiency gains when only a fraction of cases requires human attention. Still, there is no doubt that humans remain indispensable.

> **Most of it runs really well**
>
> *While Martha explains to me how 50–60 people handle mistakes due to automatization in her unit, she also recognizes that most of it runs smoothly, and only a very limited portion of cases end up with her and her co-workers. "Most of it runs really well," she repeats, "but if there weren't those mistakes and those things, then there would be no reason for us to be here, you could say."*
> *(Field notes, tax agency).*

### 3.1.1  Programming Human Behavior

Many tasks in the two agencies are tightly regulated and highly standardized and hence lend themselves well to digitalization, as these features facilitate programming or "scripting." Scripting describes the act of providing instructions to a computer: what to do, how, and when. In both agencies, however, "scripting" was also used to direct human behavior. In the agricultural agency, rules and regulations were converted into highly detailed instructions on how to perform inspections, what to look for, and how to interpret the rules. Instructions were updated regularly to match current legislation and could be 50–100 pages long. At the beginning of each season, meetings were held to introduce inspectors to this year's changes in regulations. Additionally, the intranet was used to share updates and adjustments on an ongoing basis.

In the tax agency, frontline workers also relied on instructions, or "task descriptions," which detailed all steps involved in a task, including screenshots of the digital systems needed to complete the process and tips on workarounds to deal with the most frequent challenges. As frontline workers frequently shifted between different tasks, they appreciated and relied on these task descriptions to navigate the different systems and get things done. Here too, task descriptions were updated regularly to match changing legislation, system updates, and so on. As one of the more experienced frontline workers, Catherine, explained: "Instructions have always been there. Anyone should be able to walk in from the street and complete the task" (field notes, tax agency). In an interview, frontline manager Keith explained it as follows:

> Their purpose is to ensure that you work in accordance with the law, i.e. according to the latest rules. So in principle you should—even if you have just sat down with the task the day before and done a piece of work and then have to do the same piece of work the next day—you still have to look up and then see whether there have been any changes to it, which you can work according to. You can easily see whether edits have been made to the task description, and if there haven't been any, then you just perform the task. Strictly speaking, you have to look it up and have it next to you. But I know that people don't do that. You go in and check whether anything has happened, and if it hasn't, you just move on. (interview, tax agency)

While one might expect such instructions to live quiet and untouched lives on the intranet, they played a vital role in everyday life at the offices. Our observations include numerous examples of employees using or referring directly to instructions while engaged in their work, taking care not to print them but always accessing them through the intranet to make sure they were using the most recent version. We also observed a number of meetings in which frontline workers and managers engaged in collaborative revision of instructions to make sure they were updated and easy to follow. While participants perceived this as a cumbersome task, they also took pride in this work and expressed different sentiments concerning the quality of instructions, indicating their importance.

However, even with these active efforts, our observations show that many aspects of work in the two agencies are less programmable than they may appear. For both digital systems and humans, we observed an "overflow" of activities that could not be handled by scripted actions but required reflection and improvisation. The ambition of scripting all aspects of work, whether carried out by digital systems or human actors, is a powerful fantasy, yet far from reality. In the next section, we take a closer look at some of the factors that challenge programmability and attempts at scripting and discuss how the upkeep of rules is influenced by participants' use of discretion. Again, it should be noted that our observations likely overrepresent situations where programmability is problematic or simply not possible, which makes digitalization difficult (cf. Chapter 2). The following sections should be read with this in mind.

### 3.1.2 Beyond Programmability: Dealing with Residuals

While programmability may be the order of the day for large parts of the work carried out in the two agencies, some aspects of work are still characterized by ambiguity and complexity that complicate programmability. In this section, we address how participants in our study handle this. We first show how additional informal systems are created to deal with "overflow," i.e., cases that for various reasons cannot be contained in the regular digital case management systems. We then focus on how employees handle aspects of their work that, despite all efforts, cannot be fully scripted. This concerns "back-office" aspects such as how to navigate between different digital systems as well as encounters with citizens.

> **It would be great to clear it out**
>
> *Catherine transfers numbers from one system into an Excel sheet in another system. "This piece of information is always missing," she says as she enters numbers into the spreadsheet, commenting that entering the numbers "is just as fast as copy/paste." The system is ancient and was developed for different purposes but can be used for an array of cases and events that cannot be handled by other systems, such as*

> *fines for foreigners without a CPR number, or companies without a CVR. Since the system is old and no longer fit for purpose, there is an ongoing organizational process with the aim of "emptying" the system and closing it down. Catherine is part of this process, but the challenge is that these cases do not really fit in any other systems either. "It would be great to clear it out, but I don't really believe in it," she says.*
> 
> *(Field notes, tax agency)*

"It would be great to clear it out" illustrates the need to handle cases where data is missing, or that do not conform to the requirements of advanced systems. Although they do not "fit in," these cases still exist, and the agency needs to deal with them. The system in the example is old and essentially unfit for many of the purposes for which it is currently used. This is one reason why it demands many manual processes and is unable to communicate with other systems or retrieve information from relevant registries. Ideally, this system would be emptied and closed, but the newer automated systems cannot handle the cases that are currently contained in the old system. While there is an ambition to "empty" the old system and close it down, it fulfills an important role in managing cases that do not fit in elsewhere.

Similarly, in "Clean-up duty" and "What constitutes a problem?" in Chapter 2, we see how scripted automated case processing turns out to be technically correct but legally incorrect, resulting in clean-up tasks for employees. However, beyond pointing to the inefficiency of these manual processes, which appear to be unavoidable companions to otherwise highly efficient automation, these cases also illustrate that automatization sometimes creates situations where the agency, despite all good efforts, does not administer its tasks according to the rules. In other words, digitalization and automatization generate residuals, complexity, and contingencies that employees need to handle. These "side effects" are managed by keeping old systems "alive," by employing manual processes, and by developing parallel systems, e.g., using email to manage that which is not (yet) programmed or programmable.

Employees use email for all kinds of communication, including management of cases, for example to deal with requests from citizens or pass these on to their co-workers in other parts of the organization. In our observations, it appeared that email was often used in parallel with the official case management systems. In one unit, a shared mailbox doubled as an archive for cases that had not yet been assigned to an employee. Everyone regarded this as a temporary but necessary solution for handling cases that were not properly registered in the case management system. Some employees deliberately communicate with citizens via email instead of the software they are supposed to use, for example when forwarding official documents. They explain that the designated system cannot handle large attachments, and so using the system would require them to split up, e.g., a report and its appendices into several messages—a cumbersome process for them and the receiving citizen, when the same task can be handled with just one email.

In many instances, it makes sense to use email because it allows for a high degree of flexibility in dealing with cases. In organizations that have highly scripted processes for case management as well as interactions with citizens, e.g., through self-service systems, it seems natural that there is a need for an informal space where requests and data do not have to conform to any preset standard. While some of these informal or non-standardized processes could perhaps be integrated in existing or newly developed systems or even automatized, the need for a parallel system would likely not disappear. Yet while these parallel systems can be regarded as sensible and necessary, they do not always conform to standards regarding, for example, data security—a problem of which employees and managers were well aware.

### 3.1.3  When Instructions Fall Short: The Need for a Human Touch

As noted, all back-office tasks are, in principle, scripted in as much detail as possible in official instructions and work descriptions. Yet, even if these instructions are used and appreciated in everyday practice, it is also clear that there are many cases and situations where scripts and instructions are insufficient on their own. Our observations include numerous examples of employees standing or sitting next to each other, or engaged in online meetings, with the purpose of teaching and learning how to navigate the digital case management systems. Instructions certainly played an important role in these processes, and learning how to process simple cases in a particular system often appeared quite manageable when following the detailed instructions, perhaps supplemented by a few demonstrations. What proved difficult was rather the tasks of navigating *between* the many different systems, learning how they fit together in more complicated processes, and figuring out where to find relevant information and how to integrate it, automatically or manually, into another system.

In other words, frontline workers need to learn not only how to navigate a particular system to solve a task but also how to navigate the highly complex "artifact ecology" of the digitalized public bureaucracy. This was observable in both agencies. They also had to learn the many tips and tricks for how to deal with unaccommodating or troublesome technologies, including how to "play support right" (cf. Chapter 2). While the most common workarounds might be included directly in work descriptions, or shared on the intranet, much of this is difficult to convey in writing and must be learned by asking and imitating co-workers and through practical experience (Møller 2024).

Another challenge concerned figuring out how to deal with cases that did not "fit in," where there was uncertainty regarding the interpretation of rules, or where an unknown error had occurred. As frontline manager Keith explained in an interview: "There are some cases where the errors are not known yet. You don't know what the cause of a discrepancy is, and you can't create a task description on it when you can't see what the error is at all" (interview, tax agency). These situations often required a broader and deeper understanding of how the digitalized case processes work, as well as knowledge about the routines of sister agencies, developments in related policy areas, and/or detailed insight into past and present rules and legislation.

Importantly, some processes and decisions cannot be fully programmed or automated because the law requires that individual assessments be made. Accordingly, frontline workers must evaluate cases independently and exercise discretion, taking their particular circumstances into account. In both agencies, encounters with citizens also demanded more than could be included in written instructions. We expand on these aspects of work in the following section.

Looking across our observations regarding rules and programmability, we find that digital technologies support and enable programmability of both digital systems and human activity in the two agencies. Notably, both frontline workers and managers value detailed instructions over discretion and prefer clear directions over uncertainty. Standardization, predictability, and consistency in case processing and decision-making thus appear as an integral part of their bureaucratic ethos. As we argued at the outset of the chapter, rules also reflect an institutional order, and we find this mirrored in the two agencies. Accordingly, the many situations

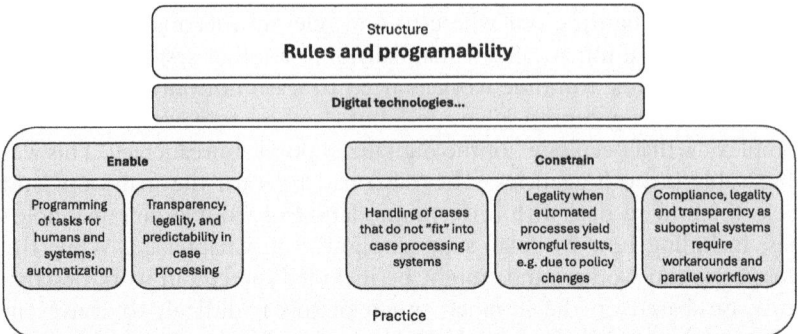

**Fig. 3.1** How digital technologies enable and constrain rules and programmability

where digital technologies constrain the programmability of tasks—because cases do not fit in, because there is a need to use more systems, or because automated processes that are essentially "correct" yield incorrect results—generate frustration and lead employees and managers to generate parallel systems, overflow systems, or workarounds. However, they are also acutely aware when such solutions are not compliant with internal rules or standards. We summarize these findings in Fig. 3.1.

## 3.2 Discretion in the Digitalized Bureaucracy

In the previous section, we studied how rules and programmability play out in the digitalized bureaucracy. While parallel systems are created to deal with "overflow" and non-standard cases, employees also need to handle other aspects of their work that for various reasons cannot be fully scripted. In this section, we dig more deeply into the question of employee discretion and what it looks like in the digitalized bureaucracy.

### 3.2.1 *The Changing Nature of Discretionary Decision-Making*

While much of the work in public bureaucracies is standardized, and many decisions in digitalized bureaucracies are automated, some types of cases require frontline employees to use their discretion. In the tax agency, some units deal only with cases that require individual judgment and decision-making. In "We make decisions," a caseworker in one such unit prepares for a meeting where she and a co-worker collaborate on revising instructions for their co-workers, although she explains that their work cannot really be formulated in instructions. In her view, the fact that they need to make discretionary decisions sets the unit apart from most other units in the agency. Still, they spend a long time working on the instructions, seeking to explicate in much detail which considerations should be included in the assessment of different types of cases while taking great care not to provide any standardized solutions or boilerplate formulations that could be copy-pasted into decision letters—as this would run counter to the requirement for individual consideration of each case.

> **We make decisions**
>
> *Joanne tells me about a meeting between her and a colleague later in the day, where they need to go through "our decisions, reasons, and management signals," she says. "Well, not really 'management signals,' but still…" I ask whether this is related to the task of updating instructions that I have heard many of her co-workers talk about. Kind of, but not really, she says, and continues: "I mean, we [in our unit] make decisions. Instructions is more about pushing this and that button, then do this and that; it is more restrictive. Some of the other units have a lot of that, where you can hand a new employee an instruction and a pile of cases and say: 'Here you go, get to work!' We don't have a lot of that—it is a bit different here. We hold our new employees' hands for months before they are let loose even a little bit."*
>
> *(Field notes, tax agency)*

In the agricultural agency, inspectors also engage in individual assessment and discretionary decision-making when carrying out inspections. Several inspectors spoke of the need to "calibrate" their interpretation of rules and individual uses of discretion. This reflects the fact that many inspections are still carried out physically. In addition to objective standards and rules, the overall assessment also relies extensively on one or a few inspectors and how they use their *senses*. Inspectors not only check the books and measure distances between property lines; they also look at animals to see whether they are fed and treated properly, they touch and shake plants to check them for pests, and they smell the stables and the fodder to detect whether something is out of order. It is difficult to script how to approach the full range of situations they may encounter, and thus inspectors need to observe and learn from each other when it comes to how to perform inspections, how to assess and handle situations, and how to interpret and apply the rules.

> **Calibrating discretion**
>
> *We are halfway through the monthly meeting for all regional team coordinators for a particular area of inspection in the agricultural agency. One of the coordinators shares experiences from their team's recent campaign, where they made targeted visits to suspected non-compliers. She explains how they teamed up "old and young" to "calibrate how we evaluate the situation" and ensure equitable judgments. It was a huge success, she says. It is "so good to stand there and look at it together." Education is always well worth it, and it also makes us faster when we are out there alone, she concludes.*
> *(Field notes, agricultural agency)*

Notably, frontline workers in both agencies appear very mindful and even proud of their role as bureaucrats and representatives of the state. In the example from the tax agency above, Joanne and her colleague spend hours discussing how they can best support their co-workers in making the legally required individual judgments on each case instead of resorting to routine assessments and the use of boilerplate language, which they perceive as a way for employees to "safeguard" themselves from making mistakes. In "Calibrating discretion," we see how agricultural inspectors are mindful of the risk of idiosyncratic judgments and seek to develop and maintain shared professional standards when faced with non-standard cases.

As agricultural inspections involve face-to-face encounters with farmers and others, inspectors are engaged in a fine balancing act between developing trusting relationships and maintaining a proper distance. On the one hand, inspectors view themselves as part of the agricultural community. They highlight the importance of meeting the farmers "at eye level," imitate their dialects to foster familiarity, and enjoy "talking shop." On the other hand, their job is to monitor and potentially sanction farmers, and their impartiality and ability to impose sanctions when needed must not be questioned, as illustrated in "Don't get too comfortable."

> **Don't get too comfortable**
>
> *Jane asks her colleague whether she has been out on inspection. Yes, her colleague says, it was almost too comfortable! We had such good chemistry. We talked about how I should not do inspections with her again. What if suddenly it [the conversation] becomes serious? Imagine sitting there drinking fruit tea and eating gingerbread and then suddenly you have to say (she clears her throat demonstratively): "You know, that fodder there, you are really not allowed to use that ...".*
>
> *(Field notes, agricultural agency)*

Traditional frontline discretion thus still plays a significant role in these highly digitalized agencies, as many cases cannot be processed without some form of individual judgment. Still, this could be about to change, enabled by digital technologies. It has been years if not decades since regular citizens were required to show up at the tax agency in person or deliver physical documentation. Today, all information needed to process cases can be found in digital systems or registries. Most citizens never encounter tax caseworkers directly, except perhaps on the telephone in rare cases.[1] Similarly, the agricultural agency is currently experimenting with so-called administrative inspections, enabled by digital technologies. On the one hand, eliminating face-to-face encounters may eliminate risk in terms of idiosyncratic uses of discretion and diminish the need for constant calibration. On the other hand, as shown in "It would be stupid to submit the evidence," inspectors highlight the difficulties of making judgments based on documents and images submitted by the farmers themselves. Still, the nature of their tasks is changing.

---

[1] There are exceptions, as some frontline workers in other parts of the agency also encounter citizens face-to-face.

> **It would be stupid to submit the evidence**
>
> *The inspectors continue to discuss the administrative unit's lack of knowledge as to how things work in the field. They have taken over fertilizer inspections. It used to be face-to-face; one would drive out and ask to see the books, then you would sit and scrutinize them, to see whether everything added up—how much fertilizer did they buy compared to how much grass was in the fields, etc. Now you send them a letter and ask the farmers to send in their books. However, the inspectors feel that the administrative staff do not always know what to look for. Sometimes, something is missing from the books, and it takes skill and experience to notice this. As one inspector remarks with a grin, "it would be stupid to submit the evidence!".*
>
> *(Field notes, agricultural agency)*

### 3.2.2 Frontline Discretion in the System-Level Bureaucracy

While some frontline workers, particularly in the agricultural agency, can still be characterized as traditional street-level bureaucrats who encounter citizens directly and exercise discretion as part of their jobs, many others do not fit this description. For these frontline workers, the majority of cases are processed automatically, and decisions typically do not concern individual cases but how to process "batches" of cases in the system—including whether and how to correct errors either manually or by adjusting the system and similar measures. These decisions do not lie with frontline workers but are negotiated in interactions involving frontline managers, process owners, and legal experts, as well as sometimes system developers, as shown in Chapter 3. In the words of Bovens and Zouridis (2002), these frontline workers are screen-level bureaucrats working in a system-level bureaucracy. While they sometimes process individual cases, their room for discretion is limited or non-existent; they simply need to follow instructions (cf. above).

It might be imagined that if frontline workers do not encounter citizens face-to-face, they need not deal with citizens' frustrations or engage in emotional labor (Guy et al. 2014). Yet even when all encounters were mediated by digital technologies, frontline workers were continually faced with citizens' reactions to administrative decisions on their taxes or debt to the state. In one unit, we observed frontline workers discussing the need to "read between the lines," meaning that they must learn to sort out all the essentially irrelevant information offered by citizens and focus only on those facts that help them figure out what rule should be applied. "Do you want my children to go hungry?" exemplifies such a situation.

> **Do you want my children to go hungry?**
>
> *Anna and Sarah are discussing a case that is to be passed on to another unit. The citizen has made a complaint about the decision made by the agency and they need to do some research on old data, which is not available in their unit. As they pass on the case, Sarah mutters "it is quite a lot [of work]." Anna interrupts: "You need to consider that it could be a lot of money for him!" Anna talks about a citizen who called her and said "my children are starving and I have to choose between dinner and paying this one." The citizen had asked her if she really thought his children should starve. And she of course did not think that, but she had to explain to him that "it is not my responsibility how you prioritize". They talk about the information they obtain about citizens in letters. Sometimes citizens write that they have been seriously ill or the like, "but I try to sort that out" Chelsea states. "The law says that they have to pay, and she had money for other things, and you can get help and stuff." Anna continues: "It is easier to leave it out, emotionally, because otherwise there are just too many emotions in this."*
>
> (Field notes, tax agency)

In this vignette, two frontline workers are explaining their professional norms to a third co-worker, who is relatively new to the job. In talking about their experiences, and the emotional strain that their natural empathy with citizens entails, they take the opportunity to clarify what in their view constitutes correct professional practice, including which considerations are and are not legitimate when dealing with citizens' cases. Their loyalty is to the law, and they have no discretion to make exemptions, even if they want to. All they can do is explain to citizens how and why they need to pay, and what will happen if they do not.

In general, we observed frontline workers trying to behave according to the bureaucratic values of legality, responsiveness, and transparency in their encounters with citizens, whether these occurred face-to-face or were mediated via emails or telephone. While dealing with written complaints can be emotionally straining, working the phones entails a more direct form of emotional labor (Guy et al. 2014). Citizens often display strong emotions like frustration, anger, or fear—some because they face severe consequences such as bankruptcy, others because they feel "lost" in the system. Some frontline workers have received threats from citizens, and conflict management and de-escalation techniques are part of their training. "Answering the phone" illustrates the work of frontline workers in the tax agency who take shifts during the day to answer phone calls from citizens and companies who have been transferred from the help desk to their unit.

---

### Answering the phone

*Martha is answering the phone today. She hands me a device that allows me to listen in on the calls, which they use for teaching newcomers. The calls come through a digital system that shows the caller's information on her screen. After each call, she has 90 seconds to make notes before the next call goes through. Usually, two people answer the phones, but if waiting time grows too long, her co-workers will drop whatever they are doing to help. Phones are a high priority.*

*The first caller has received a notification about unpaid debt but shouldn't have. Martha sees in the system that it is a mistake and apologizes, the caller seems happy, and the conversation ends. Martha knows that reminders have been sent out by mistake because they are behind on the manual corrections. She cannot remove the notification but will have to return to the case later.*

*Another caller is waiting to receive a payment from the agency. Martha looks up the case in the system and sees that the money has been transferred to the debt collection agency. "Why?" the man asks. Martha explains that if outstanding debts are registered with that agency, then the system automatically transfers the payments. "If you want to know more, you will have to talk to them," she says and helps find a phone number for him to call.*

3 RULES, PROGRAMMABILITY, AND DISCRETION ... 73

> *The calls keep coming in; most questions are related to navigating the digital self-service system. Some callers are audibly frustrated. "I will never be debt free!" one exclaims, but Martha keeps a friendly and helpful tone. Most end their calls with a sincere "thank you." In some instances, Martha must ask her co-workers for help. She then puts the caller on hold, emphasizing that she will return; they will not be transferred to someone else. Sometimes cases require a longer investigation or an answer from someone in a different unit; she then offers to call back the next day.*
>
> *Later a caller has deposited money with the tax agency, which should have been paid to another authority. Martha asks Juliet for help and together they make sure that the money is returned. "That's great," the man says before ending the call. Another caller cannot understand why his company did not receive a payment. "We have tried to transfer the money," Martha says, "but the system has put in a stop." She cannot explain why, but says that she will manually remove the stop, and then the money should be transferred.*
>
> *During a break, Martha addresses Juliet: "That guy had talked to four before me!" She explains, "I don't know why he ended up here, but I could not bring myself to transfer him once again." She explains that while it is not technically her area, she would rather look into the question herself and get back to the caller than ask him to journey on in the system, "even if it is not our task."*
>
> (Field notes, tax agency)

"Answering the phone" provides insight into some of the many different questions facing frontline workers as they seek to help citizens navigate the complex entanglement of organizational, legal, and technological aspects of their case. Some questions arise from the division of labor between different parts of the tax administration, others are created by the way automated systems work, and others again by the complexity of the tax legislation. Martha remains friendly and, in some situations, goes out of her way to respond to citizens' needs (as in the situation where the caller had talked to four people before her). This approach is shared among co-workers. As employees, they can access the digital systems of other agencies, and even if a case falls beyond their jurisdiction, they can still help callers understand what is happening in their case, or at least what information is registered in the systems. As one of Martha's co-workers explains: "I tell them what I think is happening, but I [also] tell them to call the other agency, to be absolutely sure" (field notes, tax agency).

Frontline workers in the agricultural agency also often end up helping citizens navigate the digital systems. One inspector explained how he would use his tablet not only to fill out inspection reports when out in the field, but also as a pedagogical tool during encounters, as he would take time to show farmers exactly where to find the digital form they needed to fill out, how to look up information in the digital registries, or how to use the self-service system. Digital tools may thus also enable frontline workers to enact the bureaucratic value of responsiveness vis-à-vis citizens. On the other hand, some inspectors still refrained from using digital tools during encounters or had contingency plans, e.g., arriving half an hour early to make sure that all equipment was up and running before knocking on a farmer's door. These frontline workers worried that technical failures would leave them looking like amateurs and compromise their authority as representatives of the state. In their view, digital tools were constraining rather than enabling.

Hence, while we observed many frontline workers trying to help citizens navigate the digitalized bureaucracy, it was also clear that they did not always feel satisfied with their ability to enact bureaucratic values. Our observations contain numerous examples of the frustration felt by employees when they cannot provide straight answers or feel that citizens have faced undue obstacles in their efforts to navigate the digitalized bureaucracy. We now take a closer look at how employees in the two agencies deal with these frustrations and what this reveals about their bureaucratic ethos.

### 3.2.3   Upholding the Bureaucratic Ethos

First, standardized and digitalized case processing is sometimes challenged by the fact that citizens do not always use digital technologies as intended, as shown in "Many still just write an email." It becomes part of frontline workers' job to encourage and discipline citizens to use the digital solutions available to support programmability. However, they are also aware that some citizens' apparent reluctance to do so is sometimes a reflection of how these solutions work in practice. For example, the digital system that farmers are supposed to use instead of writing emails has a history of breakdowns and technical errors. In another example, the agency has developed an app for farmers to use, and even though farmers were included in the development and testing of the app, they still experience trouble. It turns out that the app cannot be used on all mobile phones, and that it works for some of the interactions between farmers and the agency and not others.

> **Many still just write an email**
>
> *Marty explains that farmers are supposed to upload all information to the designated IT platform, "but many still just write an email." The system has been up and running for five years, he says, but some farmers just prefer doing what they have always done.*
> *(Field notes, agricultural agency)*

When citizens face difficulties navigating websites or forms for reporting information to the agencies, they may use different channels of contact, which challenges the programmability of agency responses to citizens' requests. In Denmark, all public organizations (and many private ones) use an online platform called e-books to communicate with citizens, and there are very few citizens who are exempted from using this form of digital communication. Still, inspectors are aware that farmers do not always know or use it, and so one inspector consistently ended his inspection visits by asking farmers whether they had access to their e-books and checking whether additional communication was needed to ensure that farmers would receive their report and be able to provide timely responses to any inquiries.

Citizens also make mistakes in reporting data to the agencies—sometimes on purpose, sometimes due to technical errors or misleading information on websites. In Chapter 3, "Clean-up duty" illustrates what happens when cases are missing vital information such as a CVR number. As noted, the systems are not set up to handle these non-standard cases and so they must be processed manually. Consequently, even if many tasks in the two agencies are highly "programmable" and there is a very clear regulatory basis for doing so, citizens do not always behave as intended, and digital systems cannot or have not so far been designed to handle the complexity that this generates.

At the same time, frontline workers are aware that the complexity and fragmentation that they themselves face in their work (cf. Chapter 3) also have implications for citizens. In "We are the tax agency—we should be able to explain it!" Martha is obviously frustrated by her lack of ability to provide a clear answer to a question raised by a citizen. It is clear from the example that she considers herself a representative of the tax agency and feels responsible for enacting the rule of law in the sense that citizens should be able to know what the rules are, how they are implemented, and hence what to expect. Not being able to provide the citizen with proper information due to the "black box" of automation challenges her basic assumption about the nature of her organization.

---

**We are the tax agency—we should be able to explain it!**

*One of the phone calls Martha received has sent her chasing an answer to a question raised by the citizen. She has now spent half a day trying to find the answer, even though it was not her responsibility, and the task belongs to another agency. But the citizen had talked to so many people already that Martha took it upon herself to help. She spends time consulting with co-workers but realizes that she cannot tell the citizen in what order her outstanding debts will be paid by the automated system. The matter is of great concern to the citizen because, depending on this order, her company will be declared bankrupt or not.*

*A senior co-worker advises her to let it go. Martha is frustrated: "Sometimes I really HATE this system! Do you know what I mean? Don't you ever feel like that?" She asks the senior co-worker to help and the co-worker agrees and puts her in contact with the process owners. However, even they cannot provide a clear answer, only an assumption, and so they advise her not to provide any sort of guarantee, to stay clear of any legal responsibility. Martha is discouraged by this response. Later in the day she says: "If we cannot provide an answer, then who can? We are the tax agency! We really should know and be able to explain it!".*

*(Field notes, tax agency)*

These observations indicate that many frontline workers feel responsible for not leaving citizens feeling "lost in digitalization." When technological failures, system breakdowns, and lack of transparency due to automation leave them unable to provide clarity and responsiveness to citizens, it is more than a mere annoyance: It unsettles their bureaucratic ethos. We find another example of this in "What constitutes a problem?" in Chapter 2, where Martha wonders about the response from the legal department and the risk that their decision will result in unequal treatment.

"What is acceptable?" (Chapter 2) also provides us with insight into the role of frontline workers' bureaucratic ethos and professional identity as representatives of the state. Here, employees express their embarrassment when sending out letters to citizens concerning insignificant amounts (equivalent to, e.g., 20 cents). While it is important to make these corrections in the system, as even the smallest irregularity can cause a domino effect of erroneous calculations, employees are aware that citizens will likely view this as a highly inefficient if not outright ridiculous use of government resources (notably, this concern is warranted: A Danish national newspaper recently published an article regarding a citizen who received one such claim from the tax authorities, labeling it as "absurd" and "ridiculous").[2] Similarly, in "You still have to print everything," Arnold is confronted with plant nursery owners' frustrations regarding a new digital system that they are required to use. His use of humor during this interaction and his attribution of the situation to "some lady" appears to be a way of maintaining a positive personal relationship while dealing with his own discomfort.

> **You still have to print everything**
>
> *Upon arriving at the nursery, Arnold greets the contact person in the office and hands over the certificates. She greets him in a playful tone, "So, you'll go out and approve everything?" Arnold responds with a grin. A tall man joins us for the inspection. We proceed to the warehouse, passing endless pallets of flower fertilizer before entering*

---

[2] https://ekstrabladet.dk/nyheder/samfund/absurd-renteopkraevning-paa-21-oere-jeg-var-rystet/10097895.

> *into a hall filled with plants. Arnold comments on the beautiful rosemary and engages in conversation over the different plants, as he strolls through the hall, occasionally touching plants, opening boxes and examining their contents.*
>
> *A man in black passes by and Arnold calls out to him and asks him about a meeting the day before. The man responds with eye-rolling and shares his frustrations concerning the online format as well as the topic of the meeting, namely the introduction of a new digital system to be used for exports. According to the man, the functionality of the system is far from satisfactory. Arnold listens and then, with deliberate timing, adds: "And the worst part is, the Norwegians don't accept electronic certificates, so you still have to print everything!" The man stares at him in disbelief. He then adds that the system actually works really well for imports. The man explains that as of now, they have to log in and fill out their information anew each time, because the system does not even allow them to save their basic data. Both shake their heads in dismay.*
>
> *They bid farewell and we walk back to the office. Arnold mentions the meeting to the contact person, who engages in a passionate account of her frustrations with the online meeting and the new system. She explains that she tried to get help from the agency, but the agency's designated contact person claimed that he did not know anything. "He should know more than us!" she says. Arnold repeats the fact that Norway does not yet accept electronic certificates, meaning they'll have to both use the digital system AND print for quite a while. The woman looks distressed, opening and closing her mouth. Arnold suggests it's time to get moving; they say their goodbyes and we head back to the car.*
>
> *(Field notes, agricultural agency)*

Together, these situations illustrate how employees both externalize and internalize their responses to situations where they feel that their bureaucratic ethos is challenged. Adhering to the values of bureaucracy, frontline workers sometimes seek to speak "truth to power" (cf. Chapter 1) when they encounter challenges to bureaucratic values. Yet our analysis of hierarchy in Chapter 2 suggests that it is not always clear where the power, authority, and ability to fix the identified problems resides in practice.

Overall, we find that frontline workers in the two agencies face different opportunities and requirements for exercising discretion. Some caseworkers and agricultural inspectors still function as traditional street-level bureaucrats who exercise discretion as part of their individual assessment of cases, using their professional judgment and taking into account the particular circumstances of the case when interpreting and applying the rules. However, many frontline workers operate in what Bovens and Zouridis (2002) refer to as the screen-level bureaucracy, where encounters with citizens are mediated by screens and/or telephones. Further, the cases they process are embedded in a system-level bureaucracy, where decisions do not concern individual cases but rather how "batches" of cases should be processed in the automated systems, as well as whether and how errors should be corrected. These frontline workers have little or no discretion regarding individual cases; what they can do is explain the rules to citizens and help them navigate the digital systems. They are diligent in performing this task as they seek to enact the bureaucratic values of transparency and responsiveness. In this way, digital technologies enable the development of a new form of frontline expertise.

Our examples also illustrate that while the IT systems to some extent move administrative burdens and transaction costs from the agency to the citizen (a point to which we will return in Chapter 4), there is still an acute awareness among employees that they cannot simply ignore citizens who struggle to use the digital systems, particularly because citizens' struggles sometimes reflect actual faults in the system rather than unwillingness or incompetence on the part of citizens themselves. In other words, frontline workers' bureaucratic ethos prompts them to respond to citizens in need. In discretionary interactions with citizens, digital technologies enable frontline workers by providing them with expertise in the form of privileged information that allows them to respond to citizens' needs. However, when digital technologies fail or automation results in non-transparency, frontline workers face their own limitations in responding to citizens' rights and needs. This challenges their self-perception and feelings of competence and, essentially, their bureaucratic ethos.

We summarize these findings in Fig. 3.2.

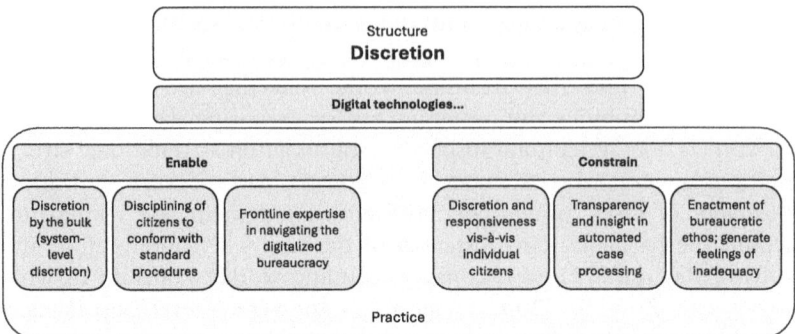

Fig. 3.2 How digital technologies enable and constrain discretion

## References

Bovens, Mark, and Stavros Zouridis. 2002. From Street-Level to System-Level Bureaucracies: How Information and Communication Technology is Transforming Administrative Discretion and Constitutional Control. *Public Administration Review* 62 (2): 174–184. https://doi.org/10.1111/0033-3352.00168.

Buffat, Aurélien. 2015. Street-Level Bureaucracy and E-Government. *Public Management Review* 17 (1): 149–161. https://doi.org/10.1080/14719037.2013.771699.

Busch, Peter André, and Helle Zinner Henriksen. 2018. Digital Discretion: A Systematic Literature Review of ICT and Street-Level Discretion. *Information Polity* 23 (1): 3–28. https://doi.org/10.3233/IP-170050.

Galbraith, Jay R. 1977. *Organization Design*. Reading, MA: Addison-Wesley Pub. Co.

Guy, Mary E., Meredith A. Newman, and Sharon H. Mastracci. 2014. *Emotional Labor: Putting the Service in Public Service: Putting the Service in Public Service*. 1st ed. London: Routledge.

Jespersen, Peter Kragh. 1996. *Bureaukratiet: Magt og effektivitet*. København: Djøf Forlag.

Lipsky, Michael. 2010. *Street-Level Bureaucracy: Dilemmas of the Individual in Public Services*. 30th Anniversary. Expanded. New York: Russell Sage Foundation.

Marienfeldt, Justine. 2024. Does Digital Government Hollow out the Essence of Street-level Bureaucracy? A Systematic Literature Review of How Digital Tools' Foster Curtailment, Enablement and Continuation of Street-level

Decision-making. *Social Policy & Administration* 58: 831–855. https://doi.org/10.1111/spol.12991.

McCubbins, Mathew D., Roger G. Noll, and Barry R. Weingast. 1987. Administrative procedures as instruments of political control. *The Journal of Law, Economics, and Organization* 3 (2): 243–277.

Møller, Anne Mette. 2024. "Re-placing interaction? Knowledge sharing among street-level bureaucrats in hybrid work settings" Paper presented at the Public Management Research Conference (PMRC), University of Washington, Seattle, WA, USA, June 26–29.

Møller, Anne Mette, Kirstine Zinck Pedersen, and Anja Svejgaard Pors. 2022. The Bureaucratic Ethos in Street-Level Work: Revitalizing Weber's Ethics of Office. *Perspectives on Public Management and Governance* 5 (2): 151–163. https://doi.org/10.1093/ppmgov/gvac001.

Olsen, Johan P. 2006. Maybe It Is Time to Rediscover Bureaucracy. *Journal of Public Administration Research and Theory* 16 (1): 1–24. https://doi.org/10.1093/jopart/mui027.

Zacka, Bernardo. 2017. *When the State Meets the Street: Public Service and Moral Agency*. Cambridge, MA: The Belknap Press of Harvard University Press.

CHAPTER 4

# The Public Bureaucracy Under Digital Transformation

**Abstract** The previous chapters have explored how central tenets of the Weberian bureaucratic model are enabled and constrained by digital technologies. In this chapter, we summarize our findings and discuss the implications of our analyses for the enactment of public bureaucratic values in practice, focusing on transparency, accountability, legality, efficiency, and responsiveness. We end with some reflections on future research into public bureaucracies in the digital age. Based on our analysis, we argue that digitalized public bureaucracies are best viewed as being under permanent reconstruction. We therefore call for a more processual understanding of digital government. Rather than a destination, digitalization is a mode of organizing that both perpetuates certain traditional organizational challenges and introduces new ones. Many of these challenges are not likely to be overcome but must be handled on an ongoing basis, and frontline managers and workers should be equipped to do so. This calls for further discussion about what kind of expertise or competences are required among frontline workers and managers in digitalized bureaucracies.

**Keywords** Bureaucracy · Digital transformation · Public bureaucratic values · Transparency · Accountability · Legality · Efficiency · Responsiveness · Expertise

Throughout the previous chapters, we have aimed to present an in-depth analysis of **how digital transformation enables and challenges the public bureaucracy and the values associated with this particular form of organization.** Based on extensive fieldwork in two Danish government agencies, we have explored how central tenets of the Weberian bureaucratic model are enabled and constrained by digital technologies, focusing on key characteristics of the bureaucratic organization, namely division of labor, hierarchy, rules, programmability, and discretion. Across our analyses, we find that digital technologies both reduce and increase the complexity of the public bureaucracy: Digital technologies enable a smoothly running bureaucratic machine while simultaneously creating snags in this machine. In this way, digital technologies play paradoxical role in their interplay with the bureaucracy.

In this final chapter, we begin by summarizing and providing some reflections on our findings from the previous chapters. We then discuss the implications of our analyses in relation to the public bureaucratic values we identified in Chapter 1, namely transparency, accountability, legality, efficiency, and responsiveness, before presenting some concluding remarks. Our study raises several questions for future research into public bureaucracy in the digital age. Here, we focus on two issues: First, we discuss what kind of expertise or competences are required among frontline workers and managers in digitalized bureaucracies. Second, we discuss the implications of an observation that cuts across the different analyses presented in this book, namely that digital technologies and digitalized public bureaucracies are under *permanent reconstruction*. We end with a call for a more processual understanding of digital government. Rather than a destination, *digitalization is a mode of organizing* that both perpetuates certain traditional organizational challenges and introduces new ones. Many of these challenges are not likely to be overcome, rather they must be handled on an ongoing basis, and frontline managers and workers should be equipped to take on this task.

## 4.1 Division of Labor

We found that division of labor expands in new directions in digitalized bureaucracies. While digital technologies enable the transparent handling of large caseloads and contribute to focusing human attention on what we could term "critical cases," we also see many instances where division of labor becomes blurred and where employees adjust their work around systems. Instances of this include situations where employees *connect* systems that do not communicate, where employees manually *rectify* mistakes made by automatic systems, and where employees *compensate* for dysfunctional systems. These activities are reminiscent of what Justesen and Plesner (2024) conceptualize as "invisible digi-work"—except these tasks are highly visible to both frontline workers and managers in our study. For many of the frontline workers we observed, this work consumes significant amounts of time and effort, but it is not something that hinders them from doing their "real" work; it *is* the work (see also Møller 2023).

These behaviors have different implications in terms of the effectiveness and transparency of bureaucracy. However, they also come with different demands for employees. Whereas the work that connects systems may demand serious attention to detail, it can still be a highly programmable task. The other types of tasks—detecting and rectifying mistakes and compensating for suboptimal digital systems—require more from employees in terms of their comprehension of systems and the legal basis for their work, as well as their industriousness in figuring out new workarounds and solutions. Moreover, these situations often require a broader and deeper understanding of, for example, the routines of sister agencies, developments in related policy areas, or detailed insight into both past and present rules and legislation. Some frontline workers and managers possess this knowledge; others rely strongly on their co-workers' or managers' insights and experience.

We also found that digital technologies challenge the traditional division of labor between different parts of the organization, and that bridging the gap between the operative core and IT functions is an ongoing task. Digital technologies allow the agencies to deal with increasing complexity both in the fields they regulate and in the ambitions of the politicians who regulate these fields. But digital technologies also increase fragmentation as the handling of cases is divided into numerous digitalized processes. Further, the need for continuous development, maintenance, and adjustment of digital solutions adds a layer of organizational complexity, as it involves several actors across different units and hierarchical layers. While they each depend on one another's knowledge and insight, their interactions often reveal the difficulties of establishing a common understanding of issues and placing responsibility for handling these issues.

Finally, we found that in ongoing discussions regarding the division of labor between humans and systems, the costs of adjusting or developing new systems are added into the mix along with considerations regarding revenue and legality. Our study illustrates how fixing problems that may impact efficiency, legality, or transparency often becomes a major task, since it involves a range of actors and ultimately demands changes in automated digital systems. Interestingly, once they are in place, digital systems tend to take on an immutable character that runs counter to the popular image of digital technologies as being highly dynamic, flexible, and adaptable. Hence, the ability to make adjustments to how cases are or have already been processed is sometimes severely limited in practice when these processes are highly automated.

## 4.2 Hierarchy

We have also examined hierarchy in the digitalized bureaucracy. Here, we found that digital technologies enable transparency with regard to access and the competences to perform certain actions, and provide a space for managers to function as experts in navigating their organization around digital systems. We pointed to the importance of controlling access to systems as a key component of managing authority in the digitalized public bureaucracy. Furthermore, we discussed how digital technologies such as email enable swift communication and facilitate transparency and accountability by making sure that managers are informed about every action and decision, yet we also noted that this "cc culture" may in fact hamper these values because of the risk of information overload. We also saw how digital technologies constrain managerial roles, as managers rarely possess the insight and expertise regarding the actual processing of cases or the workings of the digital systems. Consequently, the managerial role shifts toward *digital gatekeeping* and *digital caretaking*. Frontline managers spend a lot of their time focusing on hardware and software to ensure that employees can actually do their work.

We also find that while the bureaucratic organizational structure traditionally entails that disagreements at lower levels can be leveraged until they reach someone higher up capable of making a decision, the role of the IT organization (process owners and system developers) seems to cut across the traditional hierarchy. When observing interactions between frontline workers, frontline managers, and process owners, the "shadow of hierarchy" appears to be less present. Indeed, managers are often (and willingly) sidelined due to their lack of insight into both the technicalities of the digital systems and the daily operations of frontline workers.

Perhaps an additional factor in this is the physical dispersion of the involved actors who, in both agencies, are located not only at different hierarchical levels but also in different parts of the country and hence communicate mainly via email and online meetings. Even though they are brought together in, e.g., "construction site meetings," these meetings appear to be marked by a lack of clarity in terms of form, content, and roles, with (some) managers occupying more passive roles compared to process owners and employees.

## 4.3  Rules and Programmability

In Chapter 3, we analyzed how rules and programmability interact with digital technologies. Digital technologies enable standardization and automatization of large parts of the tasks carried out in the two agencies. Further, digital technologies encourage detailed "scripting" of non-automated tasks as well. Even the frontline workers who still exercise considerable discretion in their work prefer clear rules and programmability and value the high degree of scripting via instructions and authoritative interpretations of the rules. We hence identify a more general drive toward programmability and standardization in the two agencies, including among frontline workers whose professional identities are strongly tied to their role as bureaucrats and representatives of the state. Clear rules ensure transparency and equal treatment, which is central to their bureaucratic ethos, and function as a bulwark against discontented citizens who may direct their grievances toward the individual worker.

However, the chapter also illustrates that there are limits to standardization and the scripting of processes. For various reasons, quite a few cases cannot be handled within the available systems, and hence need employees to take on the task of figuring out what to do with them. Different parallel and more or less informal systems are created to deal with this "overflow"; some cases are stored in an outdated system that was never meant to be used for case management, others reside in designated email folders that function as "waiting lists" for cases that need someone to take care of them.

These observations underscore that even highly digitalized organizations cannot work without a human touch. We find this on many different levels. Frontline workers in the two agencies still interact directly with citizens. The controllers in the agriculture agency visit farms, they look at property lines and fences, they touch and feel flowers ready for export, and they visit stables and smell the fodder. Similarly, the employees in the tax agency pick up the phone and engage in various forms of correspondence with citizens and companies. In these situations, human competences are still needed, including emotional labor. While these employees value clear rules and regulations, their work requires them to exercise discretion, although they have very different conditions for doing so. We return to the issue of discretion below.

Beyond tasks too complex to be digitalized (as of yet), we also trace the need for a human touch in the many situations where programmability is not working or is not viable. Our material abounds with situations where systems do not function properly, where changes in the legal framework result in the need for adjustments, where citizens fail, refuse, or do not know how to use the digital systems as intended, and so on. In both agencies, we identify numerous situations where an actual person is needed to make systems work and keep processes running; sometimes due to an intended lack of system coverage, but often due to systems that were "supposed" to work but did not. Some of these gaps are considerable, as when employees in the tax agency acknowledge that they will probably still need the system they are trying to "empty," because there is nowhere else to store "misfitting" cases. Others are related to hardware, i.e., a printer that is not working or a shortage of EU-approved GPS antennae on the world market.

In sum, our analysis illustrates that while there is a powerful drive toward the standardization and programmability of all aspects of work in both agencies, and that this is strongly enabled by digital technologies, the idea that digitalization will result in "near-perfect implementation" (Bovens and Zouridis 2002) still appears to be far-fetched. Rather, we find that problems traditionally associated with standardization and programmability, including the need for parallel systems (Landau 1969), have so far survived the digital transformation.

## 4.4 Discretion

Finally, we discussed how discretion plays out. While it may have been the expectation that digital technologies would shrink discretionary room for maneuver among street-level bureaucrats (Bovens and Zouridis 2002), not least in organizations that are highly programmable, our study illustrates that there are still plenty of opportunities to exercise personal discretion for bureaucrats in the two organizations we observed. The literature on street-level digitalization generally supports this notion (Buffat 2015; Busch and Henriksen 2018; Marienfeldt 2024). Still, the two agencies differ with regard to this discretion.

In the agriculture agency, most back-office aspects of case processing have been digitalized. However, the assessment of individual cases is still highly contingent on the discretion of inspectors. While they use specific digital systems and hardware such as tablets and GPS antennae to conduct their inspections, they still use their senses—feeling, smelling, and looking at crops and animals—in their assessments. Hence, the actual assessment of cases has not been digitalized, although the agency is experimenting with so-called administrative control where farmers submit documentation digitally. Frontline workers involved in these experiments note the difficulties of making proper assessments without "being there" and are concerned about the opportunities for fraud as well as technical failure. The cases we observed clearly involved a shift of discretionary responsibilities from inspectors to IT professionals, as inspectors are not trained to tell the difference between human and technical errors and hence need the support of IT professionals to decide whether farmers should be sanctioned or not. This contributes to the blurred division of labor.

In the tax agency, most processes have been automated and only some types of (non-standard) cases, such as complaints, require individual assessment from caseworkers. The work of most frontline employees is centered on the tasks outlined above, including correcting errors and compensating for flaws in systems. In doing so, they have significant room for maneuver and perform numerous workarounds. In other words, they have a great deal of discretion in how they keep the machinery up and running but are generally not able to exercise discretion in relation to individual cases, for example during encounters with citizens on the phone. They may notice that a mistake has been made and explain this to the citizen, but they often cannot tell why, nor can they typically rectify it on their own, as automation entails that errors affect a large number of cases and must be corrected "in bulk." This requires the involvement of process owners, IT developers, and sometimes legal experts.

However, while their discretion in individual cases is limited, frontline workers still exercise discretion in deciding whether and how to help citizens navigate the digitalized bureaucracy. Our observations indicate that frontline workers in the context of digitalization take on a new role as *digital mediators* rather than expert decision-makers—a finding that is supported by other studies of frontline workers in digitalized public organizations (e.g., Pors and Schou 2021). In this role, some go above and beyond their duties and take on time-demanding *digital detective work* (Møller 2023) to answer citizens' questions and help them figure out what to do. This tendency to "move toward" citizens is well documented in the literature on street-level bureaucracy but is usually associated with the helping professions (e.g., teachers and social workers) (Tummers et al. 2015; Maynard-Moody and Musheno 2022; Lavee 2021). In taking on this responsibility, at least some of the frontline workers in our data appear motivated by a bureaucratic ethos and values pertaining to transparency, consistency and predictability, equal treatment, responsiveness, and organizational efficiency.

In sum, our findings underscore the well-established insight that ambiguity and uncertainty regarding the application of rules in everyday practice, whether by design or not, may create real struggles for public servants who need to make legislation work in practice and make sense to citizens. Against this backdrop, our analysis has shed light on how digital technologies may enable the disciplining of citizens and limit discretion, while at the same time potentially introducing additional ambiguity and uncertainty, both in the back office and during encounters with citizens. Hence the ability to help citizens may be constrained, resulting in a sense of inadequacy among frontline workers if they feel unable to enact their bureaucratic ethos.

In this discussion, it is important to highlight that most of the work carried out by digital technologies is invisible—to us as observers, but also, to a large extent, to frontline workers and managers in the two agencies, who generally deal with cases that do not "fit" into the systems, or where mistakes have been detected. This may leave us, and perhaps also the participants in our study, with the impression that most things do not work, when in fact most processes run smoothly. This implies that a key aspect of the job of frontline workers and managers is to address all the situations where the bureaucratic ethos is essentially already compromised or more difficult to attain. At least in the tax agency, frontline workers' sense of inadequacy in terms of enacting their bureaucratic ethos may thus be very clearly related to the fact that their job essentially is to "clean up" when this ethos is at risk of being, or has already been, compromised.

Based on these findings, we now turn our attention to the question of how digitalization enables and constrains the enactment of those bureaucratic values that—in ways more and less pronounced—appear to constitute the bureaucratic ethos of the people we have shadowed.

### 4.4.1 Bureaucratic Values Under Digital Transformation?

In Chapter 1, we identified five public bureaucratic values: *transparency, accountability, legality, efficiency, and responsiveness*. While as outsiders we may agree that such values are both abstract and idealized—no organization can ever honor values such as efficiency or responsiveness in all situations at all times—we find that these values are very much alive in the two agencies. They are not merely mottos, or distant abstractions to be pulled of the shelf for selected events, but are enacted in everyday practice, and we see them articulated in various situations throughout our observations and analyses. Indeed, they appear to constitute a bureaucratic ethos that (to varying degrees) motivates and guides participants in our study. This was most notable in situations where participants felt that they were not honoring this ethos. We find that employees show frustration and concern when they feel they cannot honor central values such as efficiency (e.g., when they have to work in inefficient ways), legality (e.g., when they are concerned that citizens are at risk of being treated unequally), or transparency (e.g., when they cannot tell citizens exactly how claims are processed in the automated system).

Of course, not all the observed employees and managers articulated such concerns to the same extent. Yet one central feature is prominent across the interactions we observed, namely the desire for order. Both agencies have a business to run: Inspections need to be carried out; cases and claims need to be processed. In both agencies, we find employees and managers who are strongly committed to delivering on their targets in an efficient and correct manner. In their efforts to do so, we find that *digital technologies support, enable, and amplify ambitions to ensure order and the upkeep of bureaucratic values*. Digital technologies allow the agencies to process large amounts of cases in a highly programmed way that—if done correctly—ensures transparency, accountability, efficiency, and legality. Furthermore, the division of labor between systems and humans allows humans to direct their attention to situations that are critical or unusual, or, where managers are concerned, to those that are of a more structural nature. Hence, digital technologies enable frontline workers and managers to direct their attention to the cases where it is most needed, which (potentially at least) ensures efficiency as well as legality and responsiveness.

Further, digital systems discipline managers, employees, and, not least, citizens into a framework that (ideally) reflects the legal basis and principles of sound administration on which the organizations as public bureaucracies should operate. Digital case management systems and scripted procedures for processing cases ensure that photos are geotagged, control and log who has access and which actions have been taken, pre-define formats for data input, and ensure accountability, e.g., by demanding approval by different people. In sum, we find that digital technologies enable the maintenance of the bureaucratic ethos in many ways. Participants generally recognize these enabling features and embrace the ambition and potential associated with continued digitalization. However, it is also clear from our study that digital technologies do not always deliver on their promises, and we thus also find *numerous ways in which digital technologies constrain the enactment of bureaucratic values.*

Overall, we find that digital technologies continuously increase organizational complexity, which we identify as fragmentation between organizational sub-units in our material. We find signs of parallel or cross-cutting hierarchies, including a production hierarchy, an IT hierarchy, and in some situations a legal hierarchy. Each part of the organization is necessary for the others to succeed, but we often observed that the relations and interactions between these different silos are indeterminate. In meetings, we observed difficulties in making decisions, and our material contains abundant examples of situations in which the different silos have competing understandings of what constitutes problems and solutions in any given situation.

While this is not a highly surprising finding, as decades of organization theory (Cyert and March 1963) have considered organizations to be loosely coupled entities, our findings accentuate that the increasing organizational complexity that digital transformation seems to entail also increases the resources needed for coordination, including mechanisms that mediate between mutually dependent units of the organization and ensure decisions across domains (Galbraith 1977). Hence, digitalized and automated case processing may indeed enable transparency and accountability, but may at the same time make organizations less transparent by blurring the division of labor and hierarchies of authority, which again may result in inefficiency and unclear lines of accountability.

Furthermore, just as digital technologies may support standardized and systematic workflows, they may also "mess up" and create situations where processes unintentionally become unlawful or untransparent. We observed situations where programmed actions created situations that were illegal, unfair, or difficult to "backtrack," which hampers transparency and accountability. This may be due to the features of digital systems, but is also frequently a consequence of rapidly changing rules and regulations or poor or missing data (e.g., when citizens or companies make payments to the wrong account or do not report their CVR number).

Digital technologies thus constrain the enactment of bureaucratic values in various ways. *Accountability* is easily blurred when there are cross-cutting hierarchies and more actors involved in design and decision-making and when division of labor is constantly re-negotiated, including the division of labor between humans and digital systems. *Legality* is challenged when an operation's legal basis becomes too complex for digital systems, or changes in rules and regulations are too frequent for IT developers to keep up; and the fragmentation of processes involving hardware, software, and human interaction means that few if any actors have the necessary overview or insight to detect inconsistencies and risks of unequal treatment. Errors or glitches in systems may also challenge legality, and often at a different scale than would have been the case if one employee made a mistake in one or a handful of cases.

While systems make organizations highly *efficient*, they are also extremely cumbersome to develop and change the cost/benefit analysis when considering what should and should not be fixed, or alternatively done manually. Finally, turning to *responsiveness*, digital technologies discipline citizens and the interaction between citizens and frontline workers. On the one hand, interactions become more transparent; but on the other hand, frontline workers have very limited if any room for exercising discretion, e.g., by taking individual circumstances into account, or reversing erroneous automated processes. Instead, they seek to enact responsiveness by serving as digital guides and engaging in digital detective work, yet their ability to do so is sometimes hampered by the unintelligibility of automation.

However, as Bovens and Zouridis (2002) foresaw, it is clear that discretion has not disappeared. Rather, it has shifted from frontline workers to IT developers; or more precisely, it appears to reside in the complex and indeterminate interactions between frontline workers, managers, process owners, IT developers, and legal experts, who deal with cases in "batches" rather than individually. Meanwhile, frontline discretion in relation to individual cases has shifted from decision-making to digital

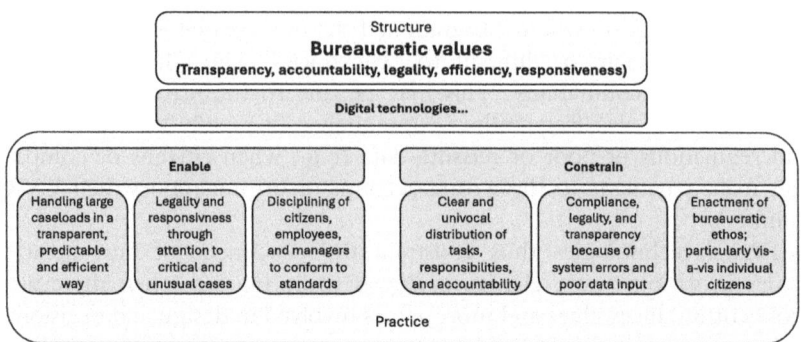

**Fig. 4.1** How digital technologies enable and constrain public bureaucratic values

mediation. While this constriction of frontline discretion is not necessarily problematic as such, our study confirms Bovens and Zouridis' concern, voiced over two decades ago, that continued digitalization could potentially conflict with public bureaucratic values, and provides a number of examples of exactly how this unfolds in practice. We summarize our findings in Fig. 4.1.

## 4.5 Concluding Remarks

We end this book with some reflections and concerns spurred by our analysis. We departed from the literature on digital transformation, and while our study clearly shows that digital competences are important (Edelmann et al. 2023), it also points to a number of additional issues that may affect the success of the digital transformation of public bureaucracies. It also raises new questions for future research into digitalized public bureaucracy.

Overall, our study points to the benefits of taking an organizational approach to the study of digital transformation in addition to focusing on individual actors (e.g., managers). Specifically, we highlight the importance of intra-organizational cooperation and the ability to ensure competent decision-making across different organizational sub-fields. However, we also illustrate how organizational complexities, such as, the legal basis on which an organization operates, the legacy of older digital systems, and the framework for managing interactions with citizens all affect the way the digital transformation of an organization plays out. Hence, we suggest that future studies of digital transformation would benefit from including a "thicker," i.e., more fully fledged, understanding of the organizational context in which digital transformations occur. This could also include more historical approaches, focusing on how current digital transformations are affected by existing organizational components as well as digital technologies already in use, existing formats of interaction between citizens and organizations, and so on.

In addition to this organizational perspective, we wish to highlight two issues raised by our analysis that may inspire future research: First, we discuss the implications of our study with regard to what kind of expertise, or competence, the digitalized public bureaucracy requires from frontline workers and managers. Second, we discuss the implications of the observation that digital technologies and digitalized public bureaucracies appear to be under *permanent reconstruction*.

### 4.5.1 Understanding Competences and Context in the Digitalized Bureaucracy

Our analyses in previous chapters suggest that the role of frontline managers in the digitalized bureaucracy is somewhat different from what we might have expected. Most notably, we find that frontline managers' expertise does not necessarily (or even typically) revolve around insight or expertise into the particular tasks of the unit they manage, nor do they necessarily possess superior expertise regarding the particular digital systems used by employees or the legislation that governs their work. Rather, their expertise lies in their ability to navigate the complex organization around digital systems and the numerous actors involved in their operation, maintenance, and development.

So far, focus in the literature on e-leadership has been on the competences needed to succeed in digitalized organizations (Van Wart et al. 2017; Roman et al. 2019). In contrast, we find that while digital competences are important for managers, including knowledge about how to steer through the helpdesk, the digital transformation of an organization does not simply add an "e-" to existing leadership competences, such as building trust; it also introduces new managerial tasks, such as guarding access to systems and ensuring that employees have adequate equipment to do their jobs. Managers in our study hence spend significant time on managing employees' access to necessary software and hardware and also take on more "janitorial" tasks, such as finding cables, testing Wi-Fi connections, or turning the power back on after blackouts. Interactions between managers and employees often focus on such tasks, and more so than on, for example, relational leadership practices (see also Winsløw and Grøn 2022).

Based on these observations, it seems pertinent to consider what kind of competences managers actually need in the digitalized bureaucracy, and whether they currently spend their time in ways that are beneficial to their organizations. Similarly, the digitalized bureaucracy seems to call for new forms of expertise among frontline workers. Bureaucrats are traditionally expected to possess knowledge and expertise that allow them to apply rules to individual cases in a consistent manner, taking any unusual circumstances into consideration. However, in the digitalized bureaucracy, frontline workers' tasks are highly programmed, determined by the setup of digital case management systems, if not completely automated. While some frontline workers still carry out individual assessments, others have little or no discretion to do so. Instead, they are developing a new form of expertise that appears to be in high demand, namely the ability to help citizens navigate the digitalized bureaucracy, which they are increasingly required by the state to master on their own. How frontline workers shape this new role as *digital mediators* deserves further investigation.

Our discussion regarding frontline workers' bureaucratic ethos and enactment of bureaucratic values in everyday practice also warrants further exploration. As we have suggested previously, not all frontline workers are alike in terms of how strongly they are motivated and guided by this ethos. Still, our observations indicate that they are often the ones who are best positioned to detect errors or inconsistencies in the digitalized processing of cases, and we have provided examples of how they seek to "speak truth to power" if they feel that public bureaucratic values are at risk of being violated. Our observations also indicate that, in some situations, it is likely that no one else would have detected the problem, due to the complex and fragmented organizational structure around digitalized processes.

In other words, frontline workers in the digitalized bureaucracy may at first sight appear merely to be small cogs in a large wheel who do not need any special skills and could eventually be replaced by robots. Indeed, automation is often associated with the de-skilling if not outright irrelevance of human labor. However, our study suggests that viewing frontline workers in this way could eventually undermine the functioning of the bureaucratic machine. Rather than de-skilling, what we observe is a process of re-skilling in which frontline workers in the digitalized bureaucracy develop new forms of expertise (see also Møller 2023). Most importantly, our study highlights the importance of having frontline workers with a strong bureaucratic ethos that prompts them to enact their unlikely yet indispensable role as guardians of the public bureaucracy.

### 4.5.2 The Production and Reproduction of the Digitalized Bureaucracy

Finally, we address an observation that cuts across all the analyses in this book, namely that digital technologies and hence digitalized public bureaucracies are in a state of *permanent reconstruction*. Our study illustrates that while digital systems may be perceived as dynamic, flexible, and evolving, they are somewhat rigid and static in nature once they are put into use. Changes to such systems often come at a high cost. At the same time, bureaucratic organizations—contrary to popular belief—are not static, and public policies, laws, and regulations even less so. Hence, the tasks of public bureaucracies and the framework in which they are supposed to perform them are constantly changing. The idea of finalizing a digital system once and for all is an illusion; as policy preferences, environmental demands, or citizen behaviors change, so must the digital systems.

What we see instead is systems that are constantly developed and changed to match the environmental complexity that the two agencies must navigate. As policy preferences change, automated processes must be adjusted, case management and self-service systems must be altered, or manual processing of claims must be put into effect. These needs may result from changes to domestic or EU legislation (which may be frequent and expected but also rapid and unexpected, prompted by external shocks like the "Britta scandal" or the COVID-19 pandemic), but they may also reflect decisions of authorities in other countries to implement new systems and procedures (this is particularly an issue for offices with international relations, such as plant export), or changes in citizens' willingness and ability to comply with the requirements of being "digital citizens."

Our data abounds with observations of ongoing adjustments to systems, both in terms of new programming and in terms of human activity "mending" holes between systems, compensating for errors, etc. These observations lead us to suggest that digital systems are never really "finished" but—just like other organizational components—may experience stability for shorter or longer periods of time before being subject to change yet again. As the Leavitt-Ry model posits, technology is one organizational variable (along with tasks, actors, and structure) that can be manipulated to ensure correspondence with environmental demands (Leavitt 1965; Nielsen and Ry 2002).

In light of this, we believe that a more processual understanding of digital systems is in order, in theory as well as practice. First, a more processual understanding could direct the attention of researchers toward the work that goes into maintaining and developing digital systems as part of everyday organizational life, rather than adopting the organizational practice of viewing and labeling such efforts as "projects"—a label that suggests that there is an end somewhere in sight. Thinking about digital technologies as infrastructure, as the literature on digital transformation posits (e.g., Cortellazzo et al. 2019), is perhaps one way of emphasizing the ongoing need for maintenance and further development.

Second, from a practical perspective, a more processual understanding that highlights the infrastructural character of digital technologies might also be beneficial in discussions about investments in digitalization, to increase attention toward the need for continuous maintenance, adjustment, and re-development. Hence, we challenge assumptions about the "finality" of digital technologies. Rather than a journey toward a complete digital transformation, digitalization is a mode of organizing that both emphasizes well-known organizational challenges and adds new ones to the mix. Many of these challenges are not likely to be overcome, but must be handled on an ongoing basis. Taking on this task requires skilled front-line workers and managers equipped with both practical expertise and a strong bureaucratic ethos.

## REFERENCES

Bovens, Mark, and Stavros Zouridis. 2002. From Street-Level to System-Level Bureaucracies: How Information and Communication Technology is Transforming Administrative Discretion and Constitutional Control. *Public Administration Review* 62 (2): 174–184. https://doi.org/10.1111/0033-3352.00168.

Buffat, Aurélien. 2015. Street-Level Bureaucracy and E-Government. *Public Management Review* 17 (1): 149–161. https://doi.org/10.1080/14719037.2013.771699.

Busch, Peter André, and Helle Zinner Henriksen. 2018. Digital Discretion: A Systematic Literature Review of ICT and Street-Level Discretion. *Information Polity* 23 (1): 3–28. https://doi.org/10.3233/IP-170050.

Cortellazzo, Laura, Elena Bruni, and Rita Zampieri. 2019. "The Role of Leadership in a Digitalized World: A Review." *Frontiers in Psychology* 10, 1–21.

Cyert, Richard Michael, and James G. March. 1963. *A Behavioral Theory of the Firm*. Upper Saddle River, NJ: Prentice Hall/Pearson Education.

Edelmann, Noella, Ines Mergel, and Thomas Lampoltshammer. 2023. Competences that Foster Digital Transformation of Public Administrations: An Austrian Case Study. *Administrative Sciences* 13 (2): 44. https://doi.org/10.3390/admsci13020044.

Galbraith, Jay R. 1977. *Organization Design*. Reading, MA: Addison-Wesley Pub. Co.

Justesen, Lise, and Ursula Plesner. 2024. "Invisible Digi-Work: Compensating, Connecting, and Cleaning in Digitalized Organizations." *Organization Theory* 5 (1), 1–26. https://doi.org/10.1177/26317877241235938.

Landau, Martin. 1969. Redundancy, Rationality, and the Problem of Duplication and Overlap. *Public Administration Review* 29 (4): 346–358.

Lavee, Einat. 2021. Who Is in Charge? The Provision of Informal Personal Resources at the Street Level. *Journal of Public Administration Research and Theory* 31 (1): 4–20. https://doi.org/10.1093/jopart/muaa025.

Leavitt, Harold J. 1965. "Applied organization Change in Industry." In *Handbook of Organizations*, edited by J.G. March. Chicago, IL: Rand Mcnally & Co.

Marienfeldt, Justine. 2024. Does Digital Government Hollow out the Essence of Street-level Bureaucracy? A Systematic Literature Review of How Digital Tools' Foster Curtailment, Enablement and Continuation of Street-level Decision-making. *Social Policy & Administration* 58 (5): 831–855. https://doi.org/10.1111/spol.12991.

Maynard-Moody, Steven, and Michael Musheno. 2022. *Cops, Teachers, Counselors: Stories from the Front Lines of Public Service. New and Expanded Edition*, 2nd ed. Ann Arbor, US: University of Michigan Press.

Møller, Anne Mette. 2023. "Inside the Digital State: Frontline Workers and Digital Transformation of Government." Paper presented at the Public Management Research Conference (PMRC), Utrecht University, The Netherlands, June 27–30.

Nielsen, J.C.R., and Ry, M. 2002. *Anderledes tanker om Leavitt—en klassiker i ny belysning*. København: Nyt fra Samfundsvidenskaberne.

Pors, Anja Svejgaard, and Jannick Schou. 2021. "Street-Level Morality at the Digital Frontlines: An Ethnographic Study of Moral Mediation in Welfare Work." *Administrative Theory & Praxis* 43 (2): 154–171.

Roman, Alexandru V., Montgomery Van Wart, XiaoHu Wang, Cheol Liu, Soonhee Kim, and Alma McCarthy. 2019. Defining E-Leadership as Competence in ICT-Mediated Communications: An Exploratory Assessment. *Public Administration Review* 79 (6): 853–866. https://doi.org/10.1111/puar.12980.

Tummers, Lars, Victor Bekkers, Evelien Vink, and Michael Musheno. 2015. Coping During Public Service Delivery: A Conceptualization and Systematic Review of the Literature. *Journal of Public Administration Research and Theory* 25 (4): 1099–1126.

Wart, Van, Alexandru Roman Montgomery, XiaoHu Wang, and Cheol Liu. 2017. Integrating ICT Adoption Issues into (e-)Leadership Theory. *Telematics and Informatics* 34 (5): 527–537. https://doi.org/10.1016/j.tele.2016.11.003.

Winsløw, Mathilde Albertsen, and Caroline Howard Grøn. 2022. ""I'm on Teams–Where Are You?"An Ethnographic Study of Differences in Leadership Practices Involving Face-to-Face and/or Digital Interaction." Paper presented at the Public Management Research Conference (PMRC), Arizona State University, Phoenix, AZ, USA, May 25–28.

# References

Anthopoulos, Leonidas, Christopher G. Reddick, Irene Giannakidou, and Nikolaos Mavridis. 2016. Why E-Government Projects Fail? An Analysis of the Healthcare. Gov Website. *Government Information Quarterly* 33 (1): 161–173. https://doi.org/10.1016/j.giq.2015.07.003.

Barrutia, Jose M., and Carmen Echebarria. 2021. Effect of the COVID-19 Pandemic on Public Managers' Attitudes toward Digital Transformation. *Technology in Society* 67: 101776. https://doi.org/10.1016/j.techsoc.2021.101776.

Blau, Peter M. 1956. *Bureaucracy in Modern Society*. New York, NY: Crown Publishing Group/Random House.

Bødker, Susanne, and Clemens Nylandsted Klokmose. 2012. "Dynamics in Artifact Ecologies." In *Proceedings of the 7th Nordic Conference on Human-Computer Interaction: Making Sense Through Design, NordiCHI'12*, 448–57. New York, NY: ACM.

Boersma, Kees, Pieter Wagenaar, and Jeroen Wolbers. 2012. "Negotiating the 'Trading Zone'. Creating a Shared Information Infrastructure in the Dutch Public Safety Sector." *Journal of Homeland Security and Emergency Management* 9 (2), 1–25. https://doi.org/10.1515/1547-7355.1965

Bovens, Mark, and Stavros Zouridis. 2002. From Street-Level to System-Level Bureaucracies: How Information and Communication Technology is Transforming Administrative Discretion and Constitutional Control. *Public Administration Review* 62 (2): 174–184. https://doi.org/10.1111/0033-3352.00168.

Boye, Stefan, Rebecca Risbjerg Nørgaard, Emily Rose Tangsgaard, Mathilde Andreassen Winsløw, and Mathias Rask Østergaard-Nielsen. 2022. Public and Private Management: Now, is There a Difference? A Systematic Review. *International Public Management Journal* 27 (2): 109–142. https://doi.org/10.1080/10967494.2022.2109787.

Boyne, George A. 2002. Public and Private Management: What's the Difference? *Journal of Management Studies* 39 (1): 97–122. https://doi.org/10.1111/1467-6486.00284.

Bozeman, B. 2007. *Public Values and Public Interest: Counterbalancing Economic Individualism*. Washington, DC: Georgetown University Press.

Brown, John Seely, and Paul Duguid. 1991. "Organizational Learning and Communities-of-Practice: Toward a Unified View of Working, Learning, and Innovation." *Organization Science* 2 (1), 40–57.

Bryson, John M., Barbara C. Crosby, and Laura Bloomberg, eds. 2015. *Public Value and Public Administration*. Washington, DC: Georgetown University Press.

Buffat, Aurélien. 2015. Street-Level Bureaucracy and E-Government. *Public Management Review* 17 (1): 149–161. https://doi.org/10.1080/14719037.2013.771699.

Busch, Peter André, and Helle Zinner Henriksen. 2018. Digital Discretion: A Systematic Literature Review of ICT and Street-Level Discretion. *Information Polity* 23 (1): 3–28. https://doi.org/10.3233/IP-170050.

Cortellazzo, Laura, Elena Bruni, and Rita Zampieri. 2019. "The Role of Leadership in a Digitalized World: A Review." *Frontiers in Psychology* 10, 1–21.

Cyert, Richard Michael, and James G. March. 1963. *A Behavioral Theory of the Firm*. Upper Saddle River, NJ: Prentice Hall/Pearson Education.

Czarniawska-Joerges, Barbara. 2007. *Shadowing: And Other Techniques for Doing Fieldwork in Modern Societies*. Malmö, Sweden : Herndon, VA : Oslo: Liber : Copenhagen Business School Press , Universitetsforlaget.

Douglas, Scott, and Albert Meijer. 2016. Transparency and Public Value—Analyzing the Transparency Practices and Value Creation of Public Utilities. *International Journal of Public Administration* 39 (12): 940–951. https://doi.org/10.1080/01900692.2015.1064133.

Du Gay, Paul. 2000. *In Praise of Bureaucracy: Weber, Organization, Ethics*. London: SAGE Publications Ltd

Dunleavy, Patrick, Helen Margetts, Simon Bastow, and Jane Tinkler. 2006. New Public Management Is Dead—Long Live Digital-Era Governance. *Journal of Public Administration Research and Theory* 16 (3): 467–494. https://doi.org/10.1093/jopart/mui057.

Durkheim, Émile. 2008. *The Division of Labor in Society*. 13. [Repr.]. New York: Free Press.

Edelmann, Noella, Ines Mergel, and Thomas Lampoltshammer. 2023. Competences That Foster Digital Transformation of Public Administrations: An Austrian Case Study. *Administrative Sciences* 13 (2): 44. https://doi.org/10.3390/admsci13020044.

Eom, Seok-Jin. 2022. The Emerging Digital Twin Bureaucracy in the 21st Century. *Perspectives on Public Management and Governance* 5 (2): 174–186. https://doi.org/10.1093/ppmgov/gvac005.

Feldman, Martha S., and Wanda J. Orlikowski. 2011. Theorizing Practice and Practicing Theory. *Organization Science* 22 (5): 1240–1253. https://doi.org/10.1287/orsc.1100.0612.

Foss, Nicolai J., and Peter G. Klein. 2014. Why Managers Still Matter. *MIT Sloan Management Review* 56 (1): 73–80.

Freudenburg, William R. 1993. Risk and Recreancy: Weber, the Division of Labor, and the Rationality of Risk Perceptions. *Social Forces* 71 (4): 909. https://doi.org/10.2307/2580124.

Gabryelczyk, Renata. 2020. Has COVID-19 Accelerated Digital Transformation? Initial Lessons Learned for Public Administrations. *Information Systems Management* 37 (4): 303–309. https://doi.org/10.1080/10580530.2020.1820633.

Galbraith, Jay R. 1977. *Organization Design*. Reading, Mass: Addison-Wesley Pub. Co.

Giddens, Anthony. 1984. *The Constitution of Society: Outline of the Theory of Structuration*. Berkeley: University of California Press.

Gulick, Luther. 1937. "Notes on the Theory of Organization" in: Luther Gulick and Lyndall Urwick. *Papers on the Science of Administration*, Institute of Public Administration, New York, NY: Columbia University, 1–36.

Guy, Mary E., Meredith A. Newman, and Sharon H. Mastracci. 2014. *Emotional Labor: Putting the Service in Public Service: Putting the Service in Public Service*. 1st ed. London: Routledge.

Hansen, M.B., and I. Nørup. 2017. Leading the Implementation of ICT Innovations. *Public Administration Review* 77 (6): 851–860. https://doi.org/10.1111/puar.12807.

Jespersen, Peter Kragh. 1996. *Bureaukratiet: Magt og effektivitet*. København: Djøf Forlag.

Jørgensen, Torben Beck. 2007. Public Values, their Nature, Stability and Change. the Case of Denmark. *Public Administration Quarterly* 30 (4): 365–398. https://doi.org/10.1177/073491490703000401.

Jørgensen, Torben Beck, and Barry Bozeman. 2007. Public Values: An Inventory. *Administration & Society* 39 (3): 354–381. https://doi.org/10.1177/0095399707300703.

Justesen, Lise, and Ursula Plesner. 2024. "Invisible Digi-Work: Compensating, Connecting, and Cleaning in Digitalized Organizations." *Organization Theory* 5 (1), 1–26. https://doi.org/10.1177/26317877241235938.

Kluckhohn, Clyde. 1951. "Values and Value-Orientations in the Theory of Action: An Exploration in Definition and Classification." In *Toward a General Theory of Action*, edited by T. Parsons and E. A. Shils, 388–433. Cambridge, MA: Harvard University Press.

Landau, Martin. 1969. Redundancy, Rationality, and the Problem of Duplication and Overlap. *Public Administration Review* 29 (4): 346–358.

Lavee, Einat. 2021. Who Is in Charge? The Provision of Informal Personal Resources at the Street Level. *Journal of Public Administration Research and Theory* 31 (1): 4–20. https://doi.org/10.1093/jopart/muaa025.

Leavitt, Harold J. 1965. "Applied organization Change in Industry." In *Handbook of Organizations*, edited by J.G. March. Chicago, IL: Rand Mcnally & Co.

Lipsky, Michael. 2010. *Street-Level Bureaucracy: Dilemmas of the Individual in Public Services. 30th Anniversary.* Expanded. New York: Russell Sage Foundation.

March, James Gardner, and Herbert Alexander Simon. 1993. *Organizations*, 2nd ed. New York: John Wiley & Sons.

Marienfeldt, Justine. 2024. Does Digital Government Hollow out the Essence of Street-level Bureaucracy? A Systematic Literature Review of How Digital Tools' Foster Curtailment, Enablement and Continuation of Street-level Decision-making. *Social Policy & Administration* 58 (5): 831–855. https://doi.org/10.1111/spol.12991.

Maynard-Moody, Steven, and Michael Musheno. 2022. *Cops, Teachers, Counselors: Stories from the Front Lines of Public Service. New and Expanded Edition*, 2nd ed. Ann Arbor: University of Michigan Press.

McCubbins, Mathew D., Roger G. Noll, and Barry R. Weingast. 1987. Administrative procedures as instruments of political control. *The Journal of Law, Economics, and Organization* 3 (2): 243–277.

Meijer, Albert, Lukas Lorenz, and Martijn Wessels. 2021. Algorithmization of Bureaucratic Organizations: Using a Practice Lens to Study How Context Shapes Predictive Policing Systems. *Public Administration Review* 81 (5): 837–846. https://doi.org/10.1111/puar.13391.

Mergel, Ines, Noella Edelmann, and Nathalie Haug. 2019. Defining Digital Transformation: Results from Expert Interviews. *Government Information Quarterly* 36 (4): 101385. https://doi.org/10.1016/j.giq.2019.06.002.

Mintzberg, Henry. 1980. Structure in 5's: A Synthesis of the Research on Organization Design. *Management Science* 26 (3): 322–341. https://doi.org/10.1287/mnsc.26.3.322.

Møller, Anne Mette. 2023. "Inside the Digital State: Frontline Workers and Digital Transformation of Government." Paper presented at the Public Management Research Conference (PMRC), Utrecht University, The Netherlands, June 27–30.

Møller, Anne Mette. 2024. "Re-placing interaction? Knowledge sharing among street-level bureaucrats in hybrid work settings" Paper presented at the Public Management Research Conference (PMRC), University of Washington, WA, June 26–29.

Møller, Anne Mette, Kirstine Zinck Pedersen, and Anja Svejgaard Pors. 2022. The Bureaucratic Ethos in Street-Level Work: Revitalizing Weber's Ethics of Office. *Perspectives on Public Management and Governance* 5 (2): 151–163. https://doi.org/10.1093/ppmgov/gvac001.

Monteiro, Pedro, and Paul S. Adler. 2022. Bureaucracy for the 21st Century: Clarifying and Expanding Our View of Bureaucratic Organization. *Academy of Management Annals* 16 (2): 427–475. https://doi.org/10.5465/annals.2019.0059.

Nicolini, Davide. 2013. *Practice Theory, Work, and Organization: An Introduction.* Oxford: Oxford University Press.

Nielsen, J.C.R. and Ry, M. 2002. Anderledes tanker om Leavitt – en klassiker i ny belysning. København: Nyt fra Samfundsvidenskaberne.

OECD. (2024). *2023 OECD Digital Government Index: Results and Key Findings.* OECD Public Governance Policy Papers, January 30. https://www.oecd.org/en/publications/2023-oecd-digital-government-index_1a89ed5e-en.html.

Olsen, Johan P. 2006. Maybe It Is Time to Rediscover Bureaucracy. *Journal of Public Administration Research and Theory* 16 (1): 1–24. https://doi.org/10.1093/jopart/mui027.

Orlikowski, Wanda J. 1992. The Duality of Technology: Rethinking the Concept of Technology in Organizations. *Organization Science* 3 (3): 398–427.

Orlikowski, Wanda J., and Stephen R. Barley. 2001. Technology and Institutions: What Can Research on Information Technology and Research on Organizations Learn from Each Other? *MIS Quarterly* 25 (2): 145. https://doi.org/10.2307/3250927.

Padovani, Emanuele, Rebecca L. Orelli, and David W. Young. 2014. Implementing Change in a Hospital Management Accounting System. *Public Management Review* 16 (8): 1184–1204. https://doi.org/10.1080/14719037.2013.792383.

Pahlka, Jennifer. 2023. *Recoding America: Why Government Is Failing in the Digital Age and How We Can Do Better.* New York, NY: Metropolitan Books.

Perrow, Charles. 1986. Economic Theories of Organization. *Theory and Society* 15 (1–2): 11–45. https://doi.org/10.1007/BF00156926.

Pors, Anja Svejgaard, and Jannick Schou. 2021. "Street-Level Morality at the Digital Frontlines: An Ethnographic Study of Moral Mediation in Welfare Work." *Administrative Theory & Praxis* 43 (2): 154–171.

Prokop, Christine, and Markus Tepe. 2022. Talk or Type? The Effect of Digital Interfaces on Citizens' Satisfaction with Standardized Public Services. *Public Administration* 100 (2): 427–443. https://doi.org/10.1111/padm.12739.

Røhl, Ulrik B. U. 2022. *Automated, Administrative Decision-Making and Good Administration. Friends, Foes, or Complete Strangers?* PhD diss.: Aalborg University Press, Aalborg.

Røhl, Ulrik B. U. 2023. Automated Decision-Making and Good Administration: Views from inside the Government Machinery. *Government Information Quarterly* 40 (4): 101864. https://doi.org/10.1016/j.giq.2023.101864.

Roman, Alexandru V., Montgomery Van Wart, XiaoHu Wang, Cheol Liu, Soonhee Kim, and Alma McCarthy. 2019. Defining E-Leadership as Competence in ICT-Mediated Communications: An Exploratory Assessment. *Public Administration Review* 79 (6): 853–866. https://doi.org/10.1111/puar.12980.

Schatzki, T.R. 2005. Peripheral Vision: The Sites of Organizations. *Organization Studies* 26 (3): 465–484. https://doi.org/10.1177/0170840605050876.

Schatzki, T.R. 2006. On Organizations as They Happen. *Organization Studies* 27 (12): 1863–1873. https://doi.org/10.1177/0170840606071942.

Schuilenburg, Marc, and Rik Peeters, eds. 2021. *The Algorithmic Society: Technology, Power, and Knowledge*. London ; New York: Routledge/Taylor & Francis Group.

Schwartz-Shea, Peregrine, and Dvora Yanow. 2012. *Interpretive Research Design: Concepts and Processes*. E-book version. New York, NY: Taylor & Francis Ltd.

Scupola, Ada, and Ines Mergel. 2022. Co-Production in Digital Transformation of Public Administration and Public Value Creation: The Case of Denmark. *Government Information Quarterly* 39 (1): 101650. https://doi.org/10.1016/j.giq.2021.101650.

Shah, Tejal, Louise Wilson, Nick Booth, Olly Butters, Joe McDonald, Kathryn Common, Mike Martin, Joel Minion, Paul Burton, and Madeleine Murtagh. 2019. Information-Sharing in Health and Social Care: Lessons from a Socio-Technical Initiative. *Public Money & Management* 39 (5): 359–363. https://doi.org/10.1080/09540962.2019.1583891.

Simon, Herbert A. 1982. *Models of Bounded Rationality*. Cambridge, Mass: MIT Press.

Tangi, Luca, Marijn Janssen, Michele Benedetti, and Giuliano Noci. 2020. "Barriers and Drivers of Digital Transformation in Public Organizations: Results from a Survey in the Netherlands." in *Electronic Government. Lecture Notes in Computer Science*, edited by G. Viale Pereira, M. Janssen, H. Lee, I. Lindgren, M. P. Rodríguez Bolívar, H. J. Scholl, and A. Zuiderwijk, vol. 12219, 42–56. Cham: Springer International Publishing.

Taskin, Laurent, and Paul Edwards. 2007. The Possibilities and Limits of Telework in a Bureaucratic Environment: Lessons from the Public Sector. *New Technology, Work and Employment* 22 (3): 195–207. https://doi.org/10.1111/j.1468-005X.2007.00194.x.

Tummers, Lars, Victor Bekkers, Evelien Vink, and Michael Musheno. 2015. Coping During Public Service Delivery: A Conceptualization and Systematic Review of the Literature. *Journal of Public Administration Research and Theory* 25 (4): 1099–1126.

Wart, Van, Alexandru Roman Montgomery, XiaoHu Wang, and Cheol Liu. 2017. Integrating ICT Adoption Issues into (e-)Leadership Theory. *Telematics and Informatics* 34 (5): 527–537. https://doi.org/10.1016/j.tele.2016.11.003.

Wang, Shu, and Mary K. Feeney. 2016. Determinants of Information and Communication Technology Adoption in Municipalities. *American Review of Public Administration* 46 (3): 292–313. https://doi.org/10.1177/0275074014553462.

Weber, Max. 1978. *Economy and Society: An Outline of Interpretive Sociology*. edited by G. Roth and C. Wittich. Berkeley: University of California Press.

Weber, Max. 1997. *Makt og byråkrati: essays om politikk og klasse, samfunnsforskning og verdier*. 2. utg., 5. oppl. Oslo: Gyldendal.

Widlak, Arjan, Van Eck Mariles, and Rik Peeters. 2021. "Towards Principles of Good Digital Administration: Fairness, Accountability and Proportionality in Automated Decision-Making." in *The algorithmic society: technology, power, and knowledge, Routledge studies in crime, security and justice*, edited by M. Schuilenburg and R. Peeters. London ; New York: Routledge/Taylor & Francis Group.

Winsløw, Mathilde Andreassen. forthcoming. *Leadership in Digitalized Public Organizations* (working title). PhD diss., Aarhus University School of Business and Social Sciences Graduate School.

Winsløw, Mathilde Albertsen, and Caroline Howard Grøn. 2022. ""I'm on Teams–Where Are You?"An Ethnographic Study of Differences in Leadership Practices Involving Face-to-Face and/or Digital Interaction." Paper presented at the Public Management Research Conference (PMRC), Arizona State University, Phoenix, AZ, USA, May 25–28.

Wirtz, Bernd W., and Steven Birkmeyer. 2015. Open Government: Origin, Development, and Conceptual Perspectives. *International Journal of Public Administration* 38 (5): 381–396. https://doi.org/10.1080/01900692.2014.942735.

Wittmann, Sebastian, Marlen Jurisch, and Helmut Krcmar. 2015. Managing Network Based Governance Structures in Disasters: The Case of the Passau Flood in 2013. *Journal of Homeland Security and Emergency Management* 12 (3): 529–569. https://doi.org/10.1515/jhsem-2014-0078.

Ybema, Sierk. 2009. *Organizational Ethnography: Studying the Complexities of Everyday Life.* Los Angeles: SAGE.

Yildiz, Mete. 2007. E-Government Research: Reviewing the Literature, Limitations, and Ways Forward. *Government Information Quarterly* 24 (3): 646–665.

Zacka, Bernardo. 2017. *When the State Meets the Street: Public Service and Moral Agency.* Cambridge, MA: The Belknap Press of Harvard University Press.

# INDEX

**A**

Access, 3, 6, 13, 47, 49, 50, 52, 55, 56, 73, 75, 86, 92, 95
Accountability, 5, 6, 11, 55, 84, 86, 91–93
Administration, 7, 8, 11, 18, 29, 73, 92
Administrative, 2, 18, 29, 59, 69, 71, 79, 89
Artificial Intelligence, 4
Authority, 9, 11, 12, 27, 28, 40, 42, 46, 48, 49, 57, 74, 79, 86, 92
Automated, 6, 7, 34, 35, 40, 58, 60, 63, 65, 66, 73, 79, 86, 87, 91–93, 96, 97
Automation, 63, 76, 77, 79, 89, 93, 96

**B**

Bureaucracy, 2, 4–11, 14, 15, 17, 21, 28, 29, 31, 38, 46, 55, 58–60, 65, 66, 70, 74, 79, 84–86, 89, 94–97

Bureaucratic ethos, 7, 11, 58, 65, 74, 77–79, 87, 90–92, 96–98
Bureaucratic practices, 5
Bureaucratic values, 5–8, 10, 11, 16, 21, 72, 74, 78, 79, 84, 90–94, 96

**C**

Case management system, 2, 3, 12, 18, 31, 51, 62, 64, 87, 92, 96, 97
Case processing, 5, 13, 17, 34, 35, 44, 55, 63, 65, 74, 89, 92
Case studies, 14
Citizen, 3, 6, 7, 12, 13, 16, 18, 29, 32, 43, 46, 53, 55, 58, 62–65, 69–77, 79, 87–97
Client, 59
Control, 2, 6, 13, 47, 49, 50, 53–55, 86, 87, 89, 92

## D

Data, 3, 5, 14–17, 19–21, 30, 32, 53, 55, 58, 59, 63, 64, 75, 90, 92, 93, 97
Decision-making, 6, 28, 37, 58, 59, 65–67, 93, 94
Denmark, 4, 16, 18, 75
De-skilling, 7, 96
Digital infrastructure, 98
Digitalization, 3–6, 13–16, 27, 30, 31, 39, 40, 57, 59, 60, 62, 63, 77, 84, 88–90, 92, 94, 98
Digital systems, 2, 5–8, 12, 13, 15, 17, 18, 29, 32, 35, 37, 39, 41, 42, 44, 47, 56, 58, 61, 62, 65, 69, 73–75, 77, 79, 85, 86, 88, 89, 92–95, 97, 98
Digital technologies, 4–8, 12, 14–17, 21, 29, 31, 37, 40, 45, 46, 53, 55–57, 60, 65, 66, 69, 70, 74, 79, 80, 84–88, 90–95, 97, 98
Digital transformation, 3–5, 7–10, 12–15, 17, 21, 84, 88, 91, 92, 94, 95, 98
Digitization, 13
Discretion, 5, 6, 16, 21, 58–60, 62, 65–71, 79, 80, 84, 87–90, 93, 94, 96
Division of labor, 5, 8, 16, 21, 27–29, 31, 35, 37, 40, 41, 45–47, 56, 57, 73, 84, 85, 89, 91–93
du Gay, P., 8–11

## E

Efficiency, 6–8, 11, 55, 60, 84, 86, 91
  inefficiency, 63, 92
E-government, 7, 14, 84
Email, 3, 12, 18, 53–56, 63, 64, 72, 74, 86, 87
Emotion, 71, 72
Emotional labor, 6, 70, 72, 88

Expertise, 3, 6–9, 27, 46, 48, 59, 79, 84, 86, 95–98

## F

Formal organization, 28, 42, 55
Frontline workers, 2, 4–7, 17, 19, 20, 30, 34, 35, 37–39, 41, 42, 44, 47, 50, 58, 59, 61, 65, 68–74, 76–79, 84–87, 89–91, 93, 95–98

## G

Galbraith, J., 28, 58, 92
Governance, 8, 14
Government, 4, 9, 13, 14, 16, 18, 35, 77
Government agencies, 4, 10–13, 16, 50, 84

## H

Hierarchy, 2, 5–9, 11, 12, 16, 21, 27–29, 40, 46, 55–58, 78, 84–87, 92, 93
Human labor, 7, 96
Humor, 77

## I

Information and communication technology (ICT), 59
Inspection, 2, 3, 8, 18, 29, 31, 33, 51–53, 61, 67–69, 74, 75, 89
Institution, 4, 5, 9, 11, 15, 16, 65
Interaction, 3, 5–7, 18, 39, 40, 43, 51, 64, 70, 75, 77, 79, 85, 86, 91–95
IT professionals, 3, 16, 38, 59, 89
IT support, 40, 50, 51

## K
Knowledge, 6, 9, 14, 39, 42, 51, 65, 85, 95, 96

## L
Law, 9–11, 58, 61, 65, 71, 76, 97
Legal framework, 7, 88, 92, 94
Legality, 5–7, 11, 38, 44–46, 58, 59, 72, 84, 86, 91, 93
Lipsky, M., 12, 59

## M
Management, 14, 63, 72
Managers, frontline, 6, 12, 17, 20, 38, 46–48, 50–55, 61, 65, 70, 84, 86, 95
Managers, higher-level, 19, 20
March, J.G., 9, 28, 92
Meeting, 3, 12, 17, 20, 35, 38–40, 42, 43, 54, 61, 64, 67, 68, 87, 92
Mintzberg, H., 9

## O
Online, 12, 17, 20, 35, 64, 75, 87
Organizational efficiency, 59, 90

## P
Policy implementation, 9, 59
Professional, 8, 9, 11, 18, 68, 71, 77, 79, 87
Public administration, 11, 13, 14, 58
Public encounter, 17
Public sector, 8
Public values, 11

## R
Regulation, 7, 18, 60, 61, 88, 93, 97
Re-skilling, 7, 97
Responsibility, 17, 35, 39, 40, 45, 55, 76, 77, 85, 89, 90
Rules, 5–11, 15, 16, 18, 21, 52, 58–63, 65–68, 71, 76, 79, 84, 85, 87, 88, 90, 93, 96

## S
Simon, H., 9, 28
Skill, 7, 96, 98
Stakeholders, 3, 12, 59
State, 68, 71, 74, 77, 87, 96
Street-level bureaucracy, 90
Street-level bureaucrats, 3

## T
Test, 15, 39, 41, 42, 75, 96
Time, 6, 7, 13, 14, 17, 32, 34, 35, 37, 40, 43, 44, 46, 49, 53–55, 67, 74, 76, 85, 86, 90, 92, 95–98
Transparency, 5–7, 11, 56, 72, 77, 79, 84–87, 90–93

## V
Values, 3, 7, 8, 10–12, 15, 21, 58, 84, 86, 90, 91, 96
Virtual, 2, 54

## W
Weberian, 9, 59, 84
Weber, M., 8–10, 27, 28
Workaround, 32, 33, 50, 61, 65, 66, 85, 89

**SPRINGER NATURE**

# GPSR Compliance

*The European Union's (EU) General Product Safety Regulation (GPSR) is a set of rules that requires consumer products to be safe and our obligations to ensure this.*

*If you have any concerns about our products, you can contact us on ProductSafety@springernature.com*

In case Publisher is established outside the EU, the EU authorized representative is:

Springer Nature Customer Service Center GmbH
Europaplatz 3
69115 Heidelberg, Germany

The manufacturer's authorised representative in the EU is Springer Nature Customer Service Centre GmbH, Europaplatz 3, 69115 Heidelberg, Germany. If you have any concerns regarding our products, please contact ProductSafety@springernature.com

Printed and bound by CPI Group (UK) Ltd, Croydon, CR0 4YY
23/03/2026
02076355-0004